contents

introduction

Whatever your tastes, there is a type of pasta to suit you and your family. If you are trying to lose weight or eat more healthily, pasta is ideal and can be invaluable as a low-fat staple of your diet. It is popular with children and you can let them eat it as often as they like since it is low in sugar, salt and fat. Plain pasta dishes, such as macaroni with butter or cheese, are excellent for people who are unwell, and more complicated dishes including meat, poultry or seafood with herbs and spices can be served when you are feeding a hungry family or you want to impress.

Popular folklore has it that Marco Polo introduced pasta to Italy in the 13th century when he brought it back from China, but there is evidence that both countries were very familiar with pasta long before his time. Some Italian historians have claimed that the Etruscans made pasta, predating the Chinese who are thought to have begun making noodles around the first century AD.

choosing ingredients

Almost any ingredient can be incorporated into a pasta dish or added to a sauce. Some of the best-known dishes, such as Classic Tagliatelle Bolognese (see page 48), Lasagne al Forno (see page 54) and Spaghetti alla Puttanesca (see page 28), have beef or seafood as the main ingredient – apart from the pasta – and you can use many different types of seafood or cuts of meat. Depending on your store cupboard, you can create your own variations on well-known, tried-and-tested recipes. Pasta is very versatile and there are many shapes and colours readily available to make an attractive lunch or dinner. You can add more or less any vegetable to a pasta dish, creating a nutritious and filling meal. This also makes sense economically, as you can use whatever vegetables are in season, which will be less expensive. Sauces can be based around popular, familiar vegetables, such as courgettes, tomatoes or onions, or you can experiment with more unusual combinations, such as pumpkin and sun-dried tomatoes. Pasta is also a very

healthy choice for vegetarians, who can add variety to their diet with different types of pasta combined with sauces or simply baked with cheese.

versatility and variety

Many pasta dishes are made with fresh beef mince, but there are plenty of other options. Fish in a creamy sauce is a wonderful al fresco summer lunch, served with fresh salad and a glass of white wine, and can be surprisingly light, depending on the type of pasta used. Scallops and crabmeat, for example, are wonderfully complemented by pasta. Eggs, raw or hard-boiled and chopped, can be added to many sauces as an alternative or in addition to meat. While there are more exotic ingredients to experiment with, cheese and cream sauces are still among the tastiest ways of serving pasta. Whatever you have in the cupboard, refrigerator or freezer – chicken, cheese, wild mushrooms or bacon – you will find a suitable pasta dish to cook for a hungry family or an intimate lunch.

Pasta is wonderfully adaptable and you can see just how flexible it is from the range of recipes in this book. Not only are there many different ways of incorporating it into a dish, but there are different colours and flavours, as well as a huge variety of sauces. You can use the same pasta shapes and very similar ingredients and still end up with totally different dishes. Pasta can be boiled, baked, added to soups, made into salads, served as a main dish or used in a side dish.

pasta

100 BEST RECIPES

LINDA DOESER

This is a Parragon Book
This edition published in 2004

Parragon
Queen Street House
4 Queen Street
Bath BA1 1HE
United Kingdom

Created and produced by
The Bridgewater Book Company Ltd,
Lewes, East Sussex

Photographer Ian Parsons
Home economist Sara Hesketh and Richard Green

ISBN: 0-75259-937-2

Printed in Malaysia

NOTE

This book uses metric and imperial measurements. Follow the same
units of measurement throughout; do not mix metric and imperial. All spoon
measurements are level: teaspoons are assumed to be 5 ml and tablespoons are
assumed to be 15 ml. Unless otherwise stated, milk is assumed to be full fat,
eggs and individual vegetables such as potatoes are medium, and pepper is
freshly ground black pepper.

The times given for each recipe are an approximate guide only.
The preparation times may differ according to the techniques used by different
people and the cooking times may vary as a result of the type of oven used.
Ovens should be preheated to the specified temperature. If using a fan-assisted
oven, check the manufacturer's instructions for adjusting the time and temperature.
The preparation times include chilling and marinating times, where appropriate.

The nutritional information provided for each recipe is per serving or per
portion. Optional ingredients, variations or serving suggestions have not been
included in the calculations.

Recipes using raw or very lightly cooked eggs should be avoided
by infants, the elderly, pregnant women, convalescents and anyone
suffering from an illness.

cooking with pasta

There is a huge range of recipes featured in this book, from exotic dishes perfect for entertaining to simple, quick and easy dishes for a family supper. Some of the ingredients used are fresh and will have to be bought especially for the dish, others can be found in most store cupboards and refrigerators. Pasta dishes can be as rich and filling as a winter stew or as light and summery as a salad. Pasta works well in soups and can add a lovely colour if you use a variety flavoured with beetroot or spinach. Italian Chicken Soup (see page 22) and Fish Soup with Anellini (see page 24) are both delicious and make an ideal summer lunch. There are many light meals featured that make great lunches or evening snacks or can be served as a preliminary dish before the main course in the Italian style. Tagliatelle with Walnuts (see page 41) has a creamy walnut flavour. There are traditional, well-known dishes, such as Spaghetti & Meatballs (see page 50) and the newly fashionable Penne with Chicken & Rocket (see page 92). Lasagne, a perennially popular dish, can be made with meat as in the Mixed Meat Lasagne (see page 56), without meat as in Vegetable Lasagne (see page 154), with seafood as in the Lasagne alla Marinara (see page 102), or you could even try the Chicken Lasagne (see page 74). Dishes such as Linguine with Clams in Tomato Sauce (see page 120) or Pappardelle with Asparagus (see page 144) are ideal for entertaining.

It is hardly surprising that most of the recipes featured here are Italian, but there are a few different dishes from Greece and France. Italian cooking varies from region to region, so many local specialities are included. There are classics from Milan, such as Minestrone Milanese (see page 16) and Tuscan Chicken Tagliarini (see page 91) from Tuscany, the olive oil capital of the world. Campania, with its wealth of vegetables and fish, is represented by Spaghetti con Vongole (see page 122), while Bologna's signature dish, Classic Tagliatelle Bolognese (see page 48), could hardly be omitted. There are also Roman dishes, such as Tagliarini all'Alfredo (see page 44), and Sicilian ones – try Sicilian Linguine (see page 58), a delicious mixture of beef, aubergines, tomatoes and olives.

There are four chapters in this book and you can mix and match the recipes. *Soups & Light Meals* suggests dishes for a lunch, starter or light evening meal. You can use many of these recipes as side dishes, adapting them according to your taste and the number of guests you are expecting. The second chapter, *Meat & Poultry*, features many dishes that would be delicious on a cold wintry night, but they can just as easily be served in the middle of summer. *Fish & Shellfish* is a great chapter for entertaining, as seafood dishes combined with coloured pasta look fabulous. Many of the recipes are very simple to make, but look as if you have spent hours cooking over a hot stove. *Vegetables & Salads* can be a lifesaver for those with vegetarian friends.

If you live in a meat-eating household and have vegetarian visitors, these dishes provide variety and colour for very little extra effort and will be enjoyed by everyone. Pasta salads are ideal for summer, providing a change from lettuce, and they make great barbecue side dishes.

health and convenience

All the recipes in this book were written with health considerations in mind and most can be easily adapted to suit different requirements as well as different palates, without losing the essence of the dish.

Pasta is very economical and it is easy to make an inexpensive and tasty dish with few ingredients, especially if you grow your own vegetables or live near a well-stocked market. If you are boiling rather than baking pasta, then it is also fast to cook, some types taking as little as 4–5 minutes. Fresh pasta cooks very fast and dried pasta takes only a little longer. You can also pre-cook pasta to use in a salad, saving more time and making a tasty summer dish.

Often the choice for many athletes and health-conscious people, pasta is healthy and nutritious. Wholemeal pasta is available, providing an alternative for the fibre-conscious. Although it is often thought to be fattening, this is untrue. It is an excellent complex carbohydrate, which releases energy steadily, and is recommended by nutritionists. On the other hand, many pasta sauces are cooked with oil and include large amounts of cheese or cream and it is these that pile on the calories. Many of the dishes featured here are suitable for a low-fat diet, while those that aren't can be adapted to suit your requirements. Substitute low-fat creams and yogurt and cook in good-quality, heavy-based or non-stick pans with little or no added fat to make these meals low in fat. Most of the recipes specify olive oil, which is high in mono-unsaturated fats and is thought to lower blood cholesterol levels, as well as having a unique flavour.

types of pasta

There are many different shapes, colours and flavours of pasta available and you may have a choice of fresh (*pasta fresca*) or dried (*pasta secca*). Pasta can be made from many different ingredients, including soft wheat, durum wheat, buckwheat, mung beans, soya beans and rice. These last three ingredients are used mainly in Asian countries. In Italy, there is variation from one region to another. Hard durum wheat is the preferred grain in southern Italy and works well for dried pasta, which has a longer cooking time than fresh. In northern Italy, fettuccine, linguine and tagliatelle are traditionally made with softer wheat flour and mixed with egg, producing pasta with a much faster cooking time.

There are about 200 different pasta shapes and about 600 different names for them. If you are lucky enough to visit Italy, you will find that a shape may have one name in one region and a different name in another. Some pasta shapes are best served with certain sauces or types of sauces, but there is nothing stopping you from substituting your own home-made pasta shapes or the ones that you prefer. Thick, creamy sauces are often best served with long ribbons of pasta, as they will just coat the strands. Seafood sauces are served with long, thin pastas, such as spaghetti or vermicelli. Vegetable sauces should be served with shells or similar shapes that will hold some sauce with every mouthful. Every recipe suggests a type of pasta, but this is not a hard-and-fast rule.

There are also different colours of pasta available as well as different shapes. You will find that the coloured varieties are most often long ribbons, but you can buy coloured fusilli (spirals) and conchiglie (shells) as well. The reddish orange of pasta flavoured with tomato is familiar to most people and is a firm favourite with children. The flavour is not strong and is usually served with a tomato-based sauce. Spinach is also frequently used as a flavouring and provides a vibrant green colour to liven up any dish. This is often paired with plain or tomato pasta for an interesting and attractive contrasting effect. Pasta tricolore is a mixture of plain, tomato and spinach. Beetroot is a less familiar flavouring than spinach or tomato, but is very attractive with a pleasant, mild flavour. Cuttlefish or squid ink provides a dramatic black for some pasta dishes, yet will not spoil the flavour of delicate sauces. Served in many expensive restaurants, black pasta can be hard to find in the supermarket and you may need to seek out an Italian delicatessen or make it yourself. Golden brown pasta can be flavoured with wild mushrooms for a real treat.

Coloured pasta looks very impressive when entertaining and is usually no more expensive than plain. A lovely way to present a pasta dish is to cook two different colours of the same type separately and place them side by side on the plate before topping with your chosen sauce. Although some dishes are made with a particular pasta, such as Classic Tagliatelle Bolognese (see page 48), you can use any colour and flavour you like. Most of the recipes do not specify a particular colour, but there are a few exceptions, such as Paglia e Fieno with Garlic Crumbs (see page 30), literally 'straw and hay'.

Some of the long, thin, ribbon-style pasta available include tagliatelle, tagliarini, fettuccine and the broader pappardelle. The best-known thin pasta is spaghetti, but there are many other types from the very fine capelli d'angelo (angel hair), spaghettini and vermicelli to the thicker bucatini. These types of pasta can often be bought fresh or dried, rolled into small 'nests'.

Many small shapes are available dried and you may also find some fresh. Conchiglie (shells), penne (quills), farfalle (bows), macaroni and fusilli (spirals) are probably the best known, but there are also many others from gemelli (twins) to strozzapretti (priest stranglers). Short, fat tubes, such as pipe and rigatoni, are also relatively easy to find and make an attractive change. Many of

these are available made from wholemeal flour and are ideal for cold pasta salads and for children, who also love alphabet and animal shapes.

Filled pasta is popular and easy, especially if bought fresh and served with a simple sauce. Ravioli (squares) and agnolotti (crescents) are well known and the easiest filled pasta to make at home. The filled shapes of plain or coloured pasta can be cooked in boiling water for a few minutes and served with a tomato and herb sauce for an inexpensive and filling meal. Tortellini are small knots of pasta and are good served with courgette and pepper or tomato sauces. Cappelletti (little hats) and caramellone (toffees) are fun shapes, good with rich tomato or creamy sauces. The best place to buy ready-made filled pasta is an Italian delicatessen, but nothing beats home-made. Try Spinach & Ricotta Ravioli (see page 158) or Chicken & Bacon Tortellini (see page 80).

Lots of very small pasta shapes are widely available for adding to home-made soups, providing both texture and substance. These include stellete (stars), anelli (rings), seme di peperone (pepper seeds) and risi (rice grains).

There are new 'designer' pasta shapes being made all the time – canned spaghetti, however nasty, is the perfect example of this. Alphabet spaghetti is still very popular among children and a range of shapes and characters has been added to this category. Dried pasta is becoming increasingly available in new shapes and many of these are ideal for fussy children and for adults with a sense of humour.

home-made pasta

Fresh pasta is available in the chiller cabinets of most supermarkets and is easy, if slightly time-consuming, to make at home. Many people prefer fresh pasta and it is worth buying if it is well-made filled pasta, which you will find at an Italian delicatessen. Dried pasta is often thought of as being more convenient, but packaged fresh pasta is, in fact, faster and easier to prepare. Some varieties of fresh pasta can take as little as 3–4 minutes to cook, while dried pasta will usually take at least double this. Some types of pasta, mainly tubular shapes, are only sold dried. Others, including lasagne, linguine, tagliatelle and fettuccine, are sold in both fresh and dried forms, offering the cook more choice.

Commercially produced pasta is made using a machine and the dough is shaped by metal rollers, which are made from Teflon or stainless steel, giving the pasta a smooth texture and appearance. Home-made machines usually clamp to the work surface and the dough can be made by hand or in a food processor.

If you choose to make fresh pasta at home, you will reap the benefits of your hard work. You should make sure that you have the appropriate equipment handy before you begin to make your dough, including the obvious things, such as clean mixing bowls, a chopping board, a sharp knife, measuring spoons and a rolling pin. There are several other pieces of equipment designed to make pasta-making easier, and some of these, such as a pasta or pastry wheel, are essential if you are making pasta with a decorated edge. Although pasta can be rolled by hand, investing in a pasta machine will save time and make the job much easier. Various attachments for different shapes are available with some models. If you are going to make ravioli, then a ravioli cutter or set of pastry cutters will be very useful, as will a ravioli tray.

cooking pasta

One of the wonderful things about pasta is that, once you have got to grips with a couple of rules, anybody can cook it. It is almost impossible to burn, and if the worst comes to the worst and something does go wrong, you can throw it away and begin again, as it is inexpensive and fast

to cook. Unfilled fresh pasta is cooked the same way as plain dried pasta, but make sure that the cooking time is reduced according to the packet instructions.

For all types, make sure that the water is boiling before you add the pasta. You need a large saucepan of water and it should be lightly salted. The general guidelines for the amount of water to use are as follows: 4 litres/7 pints of water and 3 tablespoons of salt for every 300–450 g/10½ oz–1 lb of dried or fresh pasta. This will ensure that the pasta does not stick and will not boil dry. Do not cover the saucepan or the water will boil over. Some cooks like to add 1 tablespoon of oil in the belief that this will prevent the pasta sticking, but it is not necessary. For a main course dish, allow about 150 g/ 5½ oz of fresh pasta or 100 g/3½ oz of dried pasta per person, but quantities will vary depending on the sauce.

Add all the pasta to the boiling water and stir once to prevent sticking. Return to the boil and continue to boil, not simmer, until the pasta is cooked. When ready, the pasta should be *al dente*, which means 'to the tooth', or firm to the bite. It should retain its shape, but should not feel hard in the centre. The easiest way to test it is to bite a small piece.

Drain the pasta immediately using a large colander. Rinse with boiling water to prevent sticking, if you like, or with cold water if the dish requires cold pasta. Serve immediately, tossed in butter or olive oil or with a sauce. If the pasta has to stand while you finish the sauce, toss it in a little olive oil first. Given the choice, make the sauce wait for the pasta.

Finally, remember that cooking times apply only after the water has returned to the boil, once the pasta has been added:

- Fresh, unfilled pasta will take only 2–3 minutes to cook, although some very fine ribbons may be ready as soon as the water has boiled again.
- Dried, unfilled pasta will take 8–12 minutes to cook. Refer to the packet instructions for unusual shapes or sizes and check frequently.
- Fresh, filled pasta will take 8–10 minutes to cook, while dried, filled pasta will cook in 15–20 minutes.

essential ingredients

Parmesan cheese is often added to many different pasta dishes. Choose good-quality cheese. Buy cheese fresh and in small quantities and grate it yourself just before using. Pecorino cheese is also excellent for grating, as it is hard and only a little is needed for a wonderful flavour.

Other useful cheeses include ricotta, a soft, creamy whey cheese often partnered with spinach; Gorgonzola, a piquant blue cheese; dolcelatte, a creamy, milder blue cheese; and feta, which is a Greek ewe's milk cheese.

There is a huge variety of mushrooms available and experimenting with different flavours can be enjoyable. Some are available fresh and dried and you may be lucky enough to live where they grow wild. If you pick your own mushrooms, make sure that you can identify them accurately before

cooking and eating. Cultivated white mushrooms are the type most widely available and one of the least expensive. Button mushrooms are best used whole. Chanterelle mushrooms have a delicate flavour and golden appearance. They are usually available fresh or dried and are concave. Brush off dirt rather than washing these mushrooms, as they are porous. Chestnut mushrooms are very similar and have a firm texture and strong flavour. They are ideal for adding flavour to sauces. Morel mushrooms are becoming widely used and are available fresh or dried. Leave morels soaking in salted water for 2 minutes to remove any insects, then rinse under cold running water. Pat dry with kitchen paper and use whole or sliced. Porcini mushrooms, also known as ceps, are available fresh and dried. The dried varieties are useful when a concentrated flavour is needed, as in many pasta sauces. Oyster mushrooms are sold fresh and have an attractive fluted shape. They can be used in most dishes but release a lot of moisture during cooking. Field mushrooms are large and tasty and are best served relatively plain.

Olive oil is a very important ingredient in Italian cooking, and whole or chopped olives are also used in abundance. Olive trees have been grown in the Mediterranean for over 6,000 years, making them the oldest cultivated tree in existence. Olives are available in many different colours, green and black being the most familiar. You may also find pink or violet olives or those that are a combination of colours.

Delicious sauces can be made using olives and olive oil, and black olives will add a beautiful deep colour to pasta sauces. Italian olives have exotic-sounding names, such as Rosciolo, Biancolilla and Frantoio, but most supermarket-bought olives are suitable for making sauce. Olives can be stored in the refrigerator for convenience, but should be served at room temperature. Add to dishes towards the end of cooking so that the flavour permeates throughout the sauce, but the olives retain their texture.

Olive oil is a healthy choice and has about 77 per cent mono-unsaturated fat, as opposed to some other cooking oils and butter, which can be high in saturated fats. Olive oil can be added to the saucepan before any other ingredient or can be drizzled over cooked pasta as a finishing touch. For general cooking purposes, use virgin olive oil, as this is less expensive than the finer extra virgin olive oil. Reserve your finest and most expensive extra virgin oil for dressings and finishing touches where the flavour can be properly appreciated. Store olive oil away from light in a cool cupboard.

fresh flavours

There are many different kinds of herbs and most are easy to grow in your garden or in a window box. Fresh herbs should always be used in preference to dried, where possible, as they have a much finer flavour and colour, although you will need a larger quantity. Basil is a commonly used herb in Italy and goes particularly well with tomatoes, making it the ideal herb to use for pasta sauces. A simple tomato and basil sauce will be delicious served with ravioli or as a quick and easy spaghetti sauce. It is also an essential ingredient in pesto, a Genoese sauce. Basil does not dry well, so if the fresh herb is not available, use a spoonful of pesto instead. Tarragon pairs well with chicken; use a creamy tarragon sauce with either chicken or fish. Dill and chervil are usually used with salmon, but will work well with all seafood and in pasta salads. Parsley will go well with almost anything, and particularly with chicken and fish, although it can be added as a garnish to any dish before serving. Flat-leaved parsley, also known as Italian parsley, is traditional. Rosemary has a very strong flavour and should be used sparingly, although it goes well with baked pasta dishes and adds a wonderful aroma. Sage is a natural partner for chicken and can be used sparingly

in creamy pasta sauces. Chives provide a strong flavour and attractive colour that goes well with seafood dishes with creamy sauces and strongly flavoured tomato and meat sauces. Fresh chives are far superior to dried. Oregano and marjoram are closely related herbs and traditionally flavour many meat sauces for pasta. Garlic is a must-have and is used in most dishes. Long cooking, such as roasting, gives it a mellow flavour, but do not burn it when you are frying because it will taste bitter.

Fresh vegetables in season, whether fennel, aubergines, courgettes, peppers or spinach, are the hallmark of Italian cooking. Beans and tomatoes feature widely in pasta dishes and they do not have to be fresh. Canned pulses are easier and more convenient than dried, and canned tomatoes are an invaluable store cupboard basic. Resist the urge to buy the cheapest brand, as it is likely to be watery. Canned chopped tomatoes are usually more substantial than whole ones. Other useful tomato products include tomato paste, a strong concentrate, and passata, or sieved tomatoes. When buying fresh tomatoes, look for sun-ripened specimens, which will have a sweeter, fuller flavour than those grown under glass. Plum tomatoes are traditionally used in Italy and are less watery than standard tomatoes. Sun-dried tomatoes are available in packets or bottled in oil. Reconstitute packet tomatoes with hot water and drain bottled ones. The oil from the jar may be used for extra flavouring. Sun-dried tomato paste adds an intense flavour to sauces.

Pine kernels may be used in sauces and as a garnish. They are an essential ingredient in pesto sauce. Walnuts are also widely used. *Panna da cucina* or 'cooking cream' is widely used in Italy and is more or less the equivalent of double cream. Pancetta is an Italian bacon that adds depth of flavour to many pasta sauces. It may be smoked or unsmoked and is usually quite fatty. Streaky bacon is an adequate substitute, if you cannot find pancetta.

Discover more about Italian ingredients to enhance your pasta dishes by browsing around a good Italian delicatessen. You may even be offered samples to taste!

basic recipes

vegetable stock

makes: 2 litres/3½ pints
preparation time: 20 minutes
cooking time: 35 minutes

2 tbsp sunflower or corn oil
115 g/4 oz onions, finely chopped
115 g/4 oz leeks, finely chopped
115 g/4 oz carrots, finely chopped
4 celery sticks, finely chopped
85 g/3 oz fennel, finely chopped
85 g/3 oz tomatoes, finely chopped
2.25 litres/4 pints water
1 bouquet garni

1 Heat the oil in a saucepan. Add the onions and leeks and cook over a low heat, stirring occasionally, for 5 minutes, or until softened. Add the remaining vegetables, cover and cook for 10 minutes. Add the water and bouquet garni, bring to the boil and simmer for 20 minutes.

2 Sieve, cool and store in the refrigerator. Use immediately or freeze in portions for up to 3 months.

fish stock

makes: 1.3 litres/2¼ pints
preparation time: 10 minutes
cooking time: 30 minutes

650 g/1 lb 7 oz white fish heads, bones and trimmings, rinsed
1 onion, sliced
2 celery sticks, chopped
1 carrot, sliced
1 bay leaf
4 fresh parsley sprigs
4 black peppercorns
½ lemon, sliced
1.3 litres/2¼ pints water
125 ml/4 fl oz dry white wine

1 Place the fish pieces in a saucepan. Add the remaining ingredients. Bring to the boil, skimming off the foam that rises to the surface. Reduce the heat, partially cover and simmer for 25 minutes.

2 Sieve, without pressing down on the contents of the sieve. Cool and store in the refrigerator. Use immediately or freeze in portions for up to 3 months.

chicken stock

makes: 2.5 litres/4½ pints
preparation time: 15 minutes, plus 30 minutes chilling
cooking time: 3½ hours

1.3 kg/3 lb chicken wings and necks
2 onions, cut into wedges
4 litres/7 pints water
2 carrots, roughly chopped
2 celery sticks, roughly chopped
10 fresh parsley sprigs
4 fresh thyme sprigs
2 bay leaves
10 black peppercorns

1 Place the chicken wings and necks and the onions in a saucepan and cook over a low heat, stirring frequently, until browned all over. Add the water and stir to scrape off any sediment on the base of the saucepan. Bring to the boil, skimming off the scum that rises to the surface. Add the remaining ingredients, partially cover and simmer for 3 hours.

2 Sieve, cool and place in the refrigerator. When cold, discard the layer of fat on the surface. Use immediately or freeze in portions for up to 6 months.

beef stock

makes: 1.7 litres/3 pints
preparation time: 15 minutes, plus 30 minutes chilling
cooking time: 4½ hours

1 kg/2 lb 4 oz beef marrow bones, sawn into 7.5-cm/3-inch pieces
650 g/1 lb 7 oz stewing beef in 1 piece
2.8 litres/5 pints water
4 cloves
2 onions, halved
2 celery sticks, roughly chopped
8 peppercorns
1 bouquet garni

1 Place the bones in the base of a large saucepan and place the stewing beef on top. Add the water and bring to the boil over a low heat, skimming off the scum that rises to the surface. Press a clove into each onion half and add to the saucepan with the celery, peppercorns and bouquet garni. Partially cover and simmer gently for 3 hours. Remove the meat and simmer for a further 1 hour.

2 Sieve, cool and place in the refrigerator. When cold, discard the layer of fat on the surface. Use immediately or freeze in portions for up to 6 months.

béchamel sauce

makes: 300 ml/10 fl oz
preparation time: 20 minutes
cooking time: 20 minutes

300 ml/10 fl oz milk
1 bay leaf
6 black peppercorns
slice of onion
mace blade
25 g/1 oz butter
25 g/1 oz plain flour
salt and pepper

1 Pour the milk into a saucepan and add the bay leaf, peppercorns, onion and mace. Heat gently to just below boiling point, then remove from the heat, cover and leave to infuse for 10 minutes. Sieve the milk into a jug.

2 Melt the butter in a separate saucepan. Sprinkle in the flour and cook over a low heat, stirring constantly, for 1 minute. Remove from the heat and gradually stir in the milk. Return to the heat and bring to the boil, stirring. Cook, stirring, until thickened and smooth. Season to taste with salt and pepper.

basic pasta dough

serves: 3–4
preparation time: 10 minutes, plus 30 minutes resting

This is the most basic recipe for making pasta dough by hand. You can add colourings and flavourings according to the dish (see below).

200 g/7 oz plain white flour or strong white bread flour, plus extra for dusting
pinch of salt
2 eggs, lightly beaten
1 tbsp olive oil

1 Sift the flour and salt on to a clean work surface and make a well in the centre. Pour the eggs and oil into the well, then using your fingers, gradually combine the eggs and oil and incorporate the flour.

2 Turn out the dough on to a lightly floured work surface and knead until smooth. Wrap the dough in clingfilm and leave to rest for at least 30 minutes before rolling out or feeding through a pasta machine, as this makes it more elastic. Use as required.

basic pasta dough in a food processor

serves: 3–4
preparation time: 10 minutes, plus 30 minutes resting

Pasta made using a food processor is just as good as hand-made, but takes some of the ache out of the muscles.

200 g/7 oz plain white flour or strong white bread flour, plus extra for dusting
pinch of salt
2 eggs, lightly beaten
1 tbsp olive oil

1 Sift the flour into the bowl of the food processor and add the salt.

2 Pour in the eggs and olive oil and any flavouring and process until the dough begins to come together.

3 Turn out the dough on to a lightly floured work surface and knead until smooth. Wrap the dough in clingfilm and leave to rest for at least 30 minutes before rolling out or feeding through a pasta machine, as this makes it more elastic. Use as required.

flavoured pasta

tomato pasta: Add 2 tablespoons tomato purée to the flour when making the dough and use 1½ eggs instead of 2.

beetroot pasta: Add 2 tablespoons grated cooked beetroot to the flour and use about 1½ eggs.

saffron pasta: Soak a sachet of powdered saffron in 2 tablespoons hot water for 15 minutes. Use 1½ eggs and whisk the saffron water into them.

herb pasta: Add 3 tablespoons chopped fresh herbs to the flour.

spinach pasta: Squeeze out as much liquid as possible from 150 g/5½ oz thawed frozen spinach or 225 g/8 oz fresh spinach blanched in boiling water for 1 minute. Chop finely and mix thoroughly with the flour.

wholemeal pasta: Use 140 g/5 oz wholemeal flour sifted with 25 g/1 oz plain white flour and use 2 eggs.

using a pasta machine: Cutting pasta by hand can be fun and rewarding if you have the time, but pasta machines are easy to use and save a lot of effort. There are several different models on the market to suit all budgets and most are simple and efficient. Pasta machines make ideal wedding gifts for those interested in cooking and will last for years if used and cared for correctly.

Feed the rested dough through the highest setting first. Do this several times before gradually reducing the settings until the dough is of the required thickness.

If you have a special cutter attachment, use this to produce tagliatelle or fettuccine.

A narrower cutter will produce spaghetti or tagliarini.

soups & light meals

Adding pasta to soup is not merely a way of 'padding it out' to make it go further, although it does, of course, add substance. It is an integral part of the recipe and the soup would not have the same appearance, texture and balance without it. In Italy, soup is rarely served at lunch and is usually the first course at dinner. The classic recipes here, such as Minestrone Milanese (see page 16), certainly do make wonderful starters, but they are also substantial enough to serve as a one-pot meal, perhaps with some fresh bread or rolls, for a light lunch. Pasta is the perfect choice when you are feeling in need of an energy boost, but not hungry enough for a full meal, and many of the recipes here can be prepared and cooked within 15–20 minutes.

As pasta is so versatile, the range of dishes is extensive, from the classic simplicity of Spaghetti Olio e Aglio (see page 43) to the rich creaminess of Pipe Rigate with Gorgonzola Sauce (see page 37); and from the extravagant elegance of Fusilli with Smoked Salmon (see page 33) to the comforting familiarity of Macaroni Cheese Special (see page 36). Whether you are a vegetarian or meat-eater, and whether your preferences are for ham, bacon, cheese, fish, shellfish, herbs, vegetables, mushrooms or nuts, serve them with pasta for a satisfying snack at any time of day.

minestrone milanese

serves 6   prep: 20 mins   cook: 1 hr 45 mins

This famous vegetable soup originated in Milan, but there are different versions made throughout Italy and, indeed, across the rest of the world.

INGREDIENTS

2 tbsp olive oil

55 g/2 oz rindless pancetta or streaky bacon, diced

2 onions, sliced

2 garlic cloves, finely chopped

3 carrots, chopped

2 celery sticks, chopped

225 g/8 oz haricot beans, soaked in cold water to cover for 3–4 hours

400 g/14 oz canned chopped tomatoes

2 litres/3½ pints Beef Stock (see page 12)

350 g/12 oz potatoes, diced

175 g/6 oz dried pepe bucato, macaroni or other soup pasta shapes

175 g/6 oz green beans, sliced

115 g/4 oz fresh or frozen peas

225 g/8 oz Savoy cabbage, shredded

3 tbsp chopped fresh flat-leaved parsley

salt and pepper

fresh Parmesan cheese shavings, to serve

NUTRITIONAL INFORMATION	
Calories	380
Protein	18g
Carbohydrate	63g
Sugars	12g
Fat	8g
Saturates	2g

cook's tip

It usually takes 1–1½ hours of cooking for soaked haricot beans to become tender, but this can vary depending on how long they have been stored.

1 Heat the olive oil in a large heavy-based saucepan. Add the pancetta, onions and garlic and cook, stirring occasionally, for 5 minutes. Add the carrots and celery and cook, stirring occasionally, for a further 5 minutes, or until all the vegetables are softened.

2 Drain the haricot beans and add them to the saucepan with the tomatoes and their can juices and the Beef Stock. Bring to the boil, reduce the heat, cover and simmer for 1 hour.

3 Add the potatoes, re-cover and cook for 15 minutes, then add the pasta, green beans, peas, cabbage and parsley. Cover and cook for a further 15 minutes, until all the vegetables are tender. Season to taste with salt and pepper. Ladle into warmed soup bowls and serve immediately with Parmesan cheese shavings.

tomato soup with stellete

cook: 1 hr 15 mins   **prep: 10 mins**   **serves 4**

variation

If passata is not available, use 400 g/ 14 oz canned tomatoes. Rub them, with their can juice, through a sieve before adding to the pan in Step 1.

Popular with children and adults, this soup is the perfect choice for a family supper or, served with fresh focaccia, for a light lunch.

INGREDIENTS

2 tbsp olive oil	pinch of cayenne pepper
3 garlic cloves, finely chopped	1.5 litres/2¾ pints Beef or Chicken
2 celery sticks, thinly sliced	Stock (see page 12)
3 tbsp chopped fresh	salt
flat-leaved parsley	175 g/6 oz dried stellete or other soup
12 fresh basil leaves, shredded	pasta shapes
2 plum tomatoes, peeled, deseeded	fresh basil sprigs, to garnish
and diced	freshly grated Parmesan cheese,
250 ml/9 fl oz passata	to serve

cook's tip

Use sun-ripened plum tomatoes, if possible, as they are less watery than ordinary varieties, so are more suitable for using in sauces.

1 Heat the olive oil in a large heavy-based saucepan. Add the garlic, celery, parsley and basil and cook, stirring constantly, for 3 minutes. Add the tomatoes and passata and season to taste with cayenne pepper. Cook, stirring constantly, for 10 minutes.

2 Pour in the Beef Stock and bring to the boil. Season to taste with salt. Reduce the heat, cover and simmer for 45 minutes.

3 Add the pasta and return the soup to the boil. Cook, stirring occasionally, for a further 10–15 minutes, or until the pasta is just tender. Ladle into warmed soup bowls, garnish with fresh basil sprigs and serve immediately with the grated Parmesan cheese.

tuscan bean soup

For a warming meal on a cold winter's day, this filling bean soup will satisfy even the heartiest of appetites.

INGREDIENTS

300 g/10½ oz canned cannellini beans, drained and rinsed

300 g/10½ oz canned borlotti beans, drained and rinsed

about 600 ml/1 pint Chicken or Vegetable Stock (see page 12)

115 g/4 oz dried conchigliette or other small pasta shapes

4–5 tbsp olive oil

2 garlic cloves, very finely chopped

3 tbsp chopped fresh flat-leaved parsley

salt and pepper

NUTRITIONAL INFORMATION

Calories	189
Protein	7g
Carbohydrate	24g
Sugars	2g
Fat	8g
Saturates	1g

variation

You can substitute other beans, such as haricot or butter beans, for one or both of the beans in the recipe, if you like.

1 Place half the cannellini and half the borlotti beans in a food processor with half the Chicken Stock and process until smooth. Pour into a large heavy-based saucepan and add the remaining beans. Stir in enough of the remaining stock to achieve the consistency you like, then bring to the boil.

2 Add the pasta and return to the boil, then reduce the heat and cook for 15 minutes, or until just tender.

3 Meanwhile, heat 3 tablespoons of the oil in a small frying pan. Add the garlic and cook, stirring constantly, for 2–3 minutes, or until golden. Stir the garlic into the soup with the parsley. Season to taste with salt and pepper and ladle into warmed soup bowls. Drizzle with the remaining olive oil to taste and serve immediately.

chicken soup with capelli d'angelo

cook: 20 mins   **prep: 5 mins**   **serves 6**

This unusual version of ever-popular chicken soup is easy to prepare. Serve with hot, crusty bread for a delicious light meal.

NUTRITIONAL INFORMATION	
Calories	134
Protein	10g
Carbohydrate	14g
Sugars	1g
Fat	5g
Saturates	1g

INGREDIENTS

1.5 litres/2¾ pints Chicken Stock
(see page 12)

115 g/4 oz skinless, boneless chicken
breast, cut into thin strips

3 eggs

2 tbsp chopped fresh parsley

salt and pepper

sunflower oil, for brushing

115 g/4 oz dried capelli d'angelo

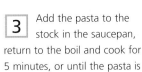

variation

Use shredded, leftover cooked chicken instead of fresh chicken and substitute the pasta with other types of soup pasta, such as anellini or ditali.

1 Bring the Chicken Stock to the boil in a large heavy-based saucepan. Add the chicken strips, reduce the heat and simmer for 10 minutes.

2 Meanwhile, beat the eggs with the parsley in a small bowl and season to taste with salt and pepper. Brush a small omelette pan with oil and heat. Add half the egg mixture, swirl the pan to cover the base evenly and cook for 2–3 minutes, or until set. Slide the omelette out of the pan and make a second omelette in the same way.

3 Add the pasta to the stock in the saucepan, return to the boil and cook for 5 minutes, or until the pasta is nearly tender. Roll up the omelettes and slice thinly. Add the omelette strips to the saucepan and season to taste with salt and pepper. Heat through for 1–2 minutes, then ladle into warmed soup bowls and serve immediately.

serves 4   **prep: 10 mins** ↺   **cook: 25 mins**

*This thick, rich soup is an ideal dish for cold, wintry evenings.
It will taste best if it is made with home-made chicken stock.*

INGREDIENTS

450 g/1 lb skinless, boneless chicken
breast, cut into thin strips

1.2 litres/2 pints Chicken Stock
(see page 12)

150 ml/5 fl oz double cream or
panna da cucina

salt and pepper

115 g/4 oz dried vermicelli

1 tbsp cornflour

3 tbsp milk

175 g/6 oz canned sweetcorn
kernels, drained

NUTRITIONAL INFORMATION	
Calories	.485
Protein	.30g
Carbohydrate	.41g
Sugars	.7g
Fat	.23g
Saturates	.13g

variation

For a chunkier version, you can use
other types of pasta, such as farfalle
(pasta bows), ruotini (little wheels) or
fusilli (spirals).

cook's tip

Always cook pasta in a large
saucepan with plenty of well
salted water. Once the water
has come to the boil, add the
pasta all at once and cook,
uncovered, until the pasta is
just tender (al dente).

1 Place the chicken in a
large saucepan and
pour in the Chicken Stock and
cream. Bring to the boil, then
reduce the heat and simmer
for 20 minutes.

2 Meanwhile, bring a
large heavy-based
saucepan of lightly salted
water to the boil. Add the
pasta, return to the boil and
cook for 10–12 minutes, or
until just tender but still firm to
the bite. Drain the pasta well
and keep warm.

3 Season the soup with
salt and pepper to
taste. Mix the cornflour and
milk together until a smooth
paste forms, then stir it into
the soup. Add the sweetcorn
and pasta and heat through.
Ladle the soup into warmed
soup bowls and serve.

fish soup with anellini

This hearty combination of fish, shellfish, tomatoes and pasta is more of a stew than a soup and would make a very filling and nutritious one-pot meal served with French bread.

INGREDIENTS

2 tbsp olive oil

2 onions, sliced

1 garlic clove, finely chopped

1 litre/1¾ pints Fish Stock (see page 12) or water

400 g/14 oz canned chopped tomatoes

¼ tsp herbes de Provence

¼ tsp saffron threads

115 g/4 oz dried anellini

salt and pepper

450 g/1 lb monkfish fillet, cut into chunks

18 live mussels, scrubbed and debearded (see Cook's Tip)

225 g/8 oz raw prawns, peeled and deveined, tails left on

NUTRITIONAL INFORMATION	
Calories	236
Protein	28g
Carbohydrate	20g
Sugars	5g
Fat	6g
Saturates	1g

variation

Other types of fish would also work well in this dish. Try cod or fresh haddock instead of the monkfish, if you prefer.

cook's tip

Buy a few more live mussels than you need for this recipe. Before you begin cooking, discard any with broken shells, or any that refuse to close when tapped with a knife.

1 Heat the olive oil in a large heavy-based saucepan. Add the onions and garlic and cook over a low heat, stirring occasionally, for 5 minutes, or until the onions have softened.

2 Add the Fish Stock with the tomatoes and their can juices, herbs, saffron and pasta and season to taste with salt and pepper. Bring to the boil, then cover and simmer for 15 minutes.

3 Add the fish, mussels and prawns. Re-cover the saucepan and simmer for a further 5–10 minutes, until the mussels have opened, the prawns have changed colour and the fish is opaque and flakes easily. Discard any mussels that remain closed. Ladle the soup into warmed bowls and serve.

serves 4   **prep: 15 mins**   **cook: 35–40 mins**

Thick, creamy and full of flavour, this is a fabulous soup for cheering you up on a cold winter's day. Serve with crusty bread.

INGREDIENTS

750 g/1 lb 10 oz mussels, scrubbed and debearded (see Cook's Tip)

2 tbsp olive oil

salt and pepper

100 g/3½ oz butter

1 onion, chopped

2 garlic cloves, finely chopped

55 g/2 oz rindless streaky bacon, chopped

55 g/2 oz plain flour

3 potatoes, thinly sliced

115 g/4 oz dried farfalle

300 ml/10 fl oz double cream or panna da cucina

1 tbsp lemon juice

2 egg yolks

2 tbsp finely chopped fresh parsley, to garnish

NUTRITIONAL INFORMATION	
Calories	.933
Protein	.23g
Carbohydrate	.57g
Sugars	.6g
Fat	.70g
Saturates	.39g

variation

Substitute the rindless streaky bacon with the same amount of pancetta and replace the dried farfalle with either fusilli or conchiglie, if you like.

cook's tip

To prepare mussels, scrub or scrape the shells and pull out any beards that are attached to them. Discard any with broken shells or that refuse to close when tapped with a knife.

1 Bring a large heavy-based saucepan of water to the boil. Add the mussels and olive oil and season to taste with pepper. Cover tightly and cook over a high heat for 5 minutes, or until the mussels have opened. Remove the mussels with a slotted spoon, discarding any that remain closed. Sieve the cooking liquid and reserve

1.2 litres/2 pints. Remove the mussels from their shells and reserve until required.

2 Melt the butter in a clean saucepan. Add the bacon, onion and garlic and cook over a low heat, stirring occasionally, for 5 minutes. Stir in the flour and cook, stirring, for 1 minute. Gradually stir in all but

2 tablespoons of the reserved cooking liquid and bring to the boil, stirring constantly. Add the potato slices and simmer for 5 minutes. Add the pasta and simmer for a further 10 minutes.

3 Stir in the cream and lemon juice and season to taste with salt and pepper. Add the mussels. Mix the egg

yolks and the remaining mussel cooking liquid together, then stir the mixture into the soup and cook for 4 minutes, until thickened.

4 Ladle the soup into warmed soup bowls, garnish with chopped parsley and serve immediately.

spaghetti alla puttanesca

serves 4 | **prep: 10 mins** | **cook: 35–40 mins**

Simplicity itself, this speedy store cupboard dish makes a really tasty lunch or light supper when you are in a hurry.

INGREDIENTS

3 tbsp olive oil

2 garlic cloves, finely chopped

10 canned anchovy fillets, drained and chopped

140 g/5 oz black olives, stoned and chopped

1 tbsp capers, drained and rinsed

450 g/1 lb plum tomatoes, peeled, deseeded and chopped

pinch of cayenne pepper

salt

400 g/14 oz dried spaghetti

2 tbsp chopped fresh parsley, to garnish (optional)

NUTRITIONAL INFORMATION

Calories 485

Protein 15g

Carbohydrate 78g

Sugars 7g

Fat 15g

Saturates 2g

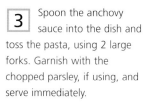

variation

You can substitute 400 g/ 14 oz canned chopped tomatoes and their can juices for the fresh tomatoes, if you prefer.

1 Heat the olive oil in a heavy-based frying pan. Add the garlic and cook over a low heat, stirring frequently, for 2 minutes. Add the anchovies and mash them to a pulp with a fork. Add the olives, capers and tomatoes and season to taste with cayenne pepper. Cover and simmer for 25 minutes.

2 Meanwhile, bring a large heavy-based saucepan of lightly salted water to the boil. Add the pasta, return to the boil and cook for 8–10 minutes, or until tender but still firm to the bite. Drain well and transfer to a warmed serving dish.

3 Spoon the anchovy sauce into the dish and toss the pasta, using 2 large forks. Garnish with the chopped parsley, if using, and serve immediately.

pasta with prosciutto

 cook: 15 mins   **prep: 10 mins**   **serves 4**

Rich and subtle in flavour and very quick to prepare, this dish would make an excellent choice for an informal dinner party.

NUTRITIONAL INFORMATION	
Calories	700
Protein	25g
Carbohydrate	65g
Sugars	6g
Fat	38g
Saturates	23g

INGREDIENTS

115 g/4 oz prosciutto

55 g/2 oz unsalted butter

1 small onion, finely chopped

salt and pepper

350 g/12 oz dried green and
white tagliatelle

150 ml/5 fl oz double cream or
panna da cucina

55 g/2 oz freshly grated
Parmesan cheese

cook's tip

Prosciutto is an Italian dry-cured ham. The best-known variety is Parma ham, but other areas produce their own types. *Prosciutto di San Daniele* is strong, while hams from Veneto have a delicate flavour.

1 Trim off the fat from the prosciutto, then finely chop both the fat and the lean meat, keeping them separate. Melt the butter in a heavy-based frying pan. Add the prosciutto fat and onion and cook over a low heat, stirring occasionally, for 10 minutes.

2 Meanwhile, bring a large heavy-based saucepan of lightly salted water to the boil. Add the pasta, return to the boil and cook for 8–10 minutes, or until tender but still firm to the bite.

3 Add the lean prosciutto to the frying pan and cook, stirring occasionally, for 2 minutes. Stir in the cream, then season to taste with pepper and heat through gently. Drain the pasta and transfer to a warmed serving dish. Add the prosciutto mixture and toss well, then stir in the grated Parmesan cheese. Serve immediately.

paglia e fieno with garlic crumbs

serves 4   **prep: 10 mins** ⟅   **cook: 10 mins** ⟅

This tasty, classic combination of pasta, pine kernels and cheese is incredibly easy to make and is ideal if you are in a hurry.

INGREDIENTS

350 g/12 oz fresh white breadcrumbs

4 tbsp finely chopped fresh

flat-leaved parsley

1 tbsp snipped fresh chives

2 tbsp finely chopped fresh

sweet marjoram

3 tbsp olive oil, plus extra to serve

3–4 garlic cloves, finely chopped

55 g/2 oz pine kernels

salt and pepper

450 g/1 lb fresh paglia e fieno

55 g/2 oz freshly grated

pecorino cheese, to serve

NUTRITIONAL INFORMATION	
Calories	.788
Protein	.27g
Carbohydrate	.113g
Sugars	.6g
Fat	.28g
Saturates	.5g

variation

For a spicy version of this dish, add 1–2 teaspoons crushed, dried chillies to the breadcrumb mixture in Step 1.

cook's tip

Pecorino cheese is an Italian hard cheese, made from ewe's milk. Pecorino Romano, from central and southern Italy, is widely available. Other varieties include Peperino Sardo and Sardo extra mature.

1 Mix the breadcrumbs, parsley, chives and marjoram together in a small bowl. Heat the olive oil in a large heavy-based frying pan. Add the breadcrumb mixture and the garlic and pine kernels, season to taste with salt and pepper and cook over a low heat, stirring constantly, for 5 minutes, or until the breadcrumbs

become golden, but not crisp. Remove the frying pan from the heat and cover to keep warm.

2 Bring a large heavy-based saucepan of lightly salted water to the boil. Add the pasta, return to the boil and cook for 4–5 minutes, or until tender but still firm to the bite.

3 Drain the pasta and transfer to a warmed serving dish. Drizzle with 2–3 tablespoons of olive oil and toss to mix. Add the garlic breadcrumbs and toss again. Serve immediately with the grated pecorino cheese.

spaghetti alla carbonara

serves 4　　　　　**prep: 10 mins** 🕒　　　　　**cook: 10 mins** 🕒

The trick is to keep everything hot, so that when you add the eggs at the end, they just cook in the residual heat, but do not scramble.

INGREDIENTS

450 g/1 lb dried spaghetti

1 tbsp olive oil

225 g/8 oz rindless pancetta or streaky bacon, chopped

4 eggs

5 tbsp single cream

salt and pepper

2 tbsp freshly grated Parmesan cheese

NUTRITIONAL INFORMATION

Calories	.709
Protein	.32g
Carbohydrate	.84g
Sugars	.5g
Fat	.30g
Saturates	.10g

variation

For a more substantial dish, cook 1–2 finely chopped shallots with the pancetta and add 115 g/4 oz sliced mushrooms after 4 minutes.

1 Bring a large heavy-based saucepan of lightly salted water to the boil. Add the pasta, return to the boil and cook for 8–10 minutes, or until tender but still firm to the bite.

2 Meanwhile, heat the olive oil in a heavy-based frying pan. Add the pancetta strips and cook over a medium heat, stirring frequently, for 8–10 minutes.

3 Beat the eggs with the cream in a small bowl and season to taste with salt and pepper. Drain the pasta and return it to the saucepan. Tip in the contents of the frying pan, then add the egg mixture and half the Parmesan cheese. Stir well, then transfer to a warmed serving dish. Serve immediately, sprinkled with the remaining cheese.

fusilli with smoked salmon

⏲ **cook: 10–12 mins**   ⏱ **prep: 10 mins**   **serves 4**

Simple and elegant, this dish provides a taste of luxury that is irresistible. Serve as a starter or add a salad to make a main course.

NUTRITIONAL INFORMATION

Calories	1064
Protein	. . . . .30g
Carbohydrate	. . . . .88g
Sugars	. . . . .8g
Fat	. . . . .67g
Saturates	. . . . .40g

INGREDIENTS

450 g/1 lb dried fusilli

55 g/2 oz unsalted butter

1 small onion, finely chopped

6 tbsp dry white wine

425 ml/15 fl oz double cream

salt and pepper

225 g/8 oz smoked salmon

2 tbsp snipped fresh dill

1–2 tbsp lemon juice

TO GARNISH

½ lemon

fresh dill sprig

cook's tip

Smoked salmon offcuts and misshapen pieces are much less expensive than slices and work perfectly well in this dish.

1 Bring a large heavy-based saucepan of lightly salted water to the boil. Add the pasta, return to the boil and cook for 8–10 minutes, or until tender but still firm to the bite.

2 Meanwhile, melt the butter in a heavy-based saucepan. Add the onion and cook over a low heat, stirring occasionally, for 5 minutes, or until softened. Add the wine, bring to the boil and continue boiling until reduced by two-thirds. Pour in the cream and season to taste with salt and pepper. Bring to the boil, reduce the heat and simmer for 2 minutes, or until slightly thickened. Cut the smoked salmon into squares and stir into the saucepan with the dill and lemon juice to taste.

3 Drain the pasta and transfer to a warmed serving dish. Add the smoked salmon mixture and toss well. Cut the top part of the rind of the lemon half into a spiral shape, and place the lemon half on top of the pasta to garnish. Add a dill sprig and serve.

spicy mushroom pasta

🍳 **cook: 1 hr 15 mins**   ⏲ **prep: 10 mins**   **serves 4**

NUTRITIONAL INFORMATION

Calories 598

Protein 15g

Carbohydrate 84g

Sugars 8g

Fat 22g

Saturates 5g

variation

If you prefer a milder flavour, reduce the number of chillies. Alternatively, omit Step 2 completely and serve the penne with the mushroom sauce.

This richly flavoured sauce would go very well with any type of short pasta, such as fusilli, conchiglie or even orecchiette.

INGREDIENTS

15 g/½ oz butter

6 tbsp olive oil

225 g/8 oz wild mushrooms, sliced

25 g/1 oz plain flour

200 ml/7 fl oz Beef Stock (see page 12)

150 ml/5 fl oz full-bodied red wine

4 tomatoes, peeled and chopped

1 tbsp tomato purée

1 tsp sugar

1 tbsp shredded fresh basil

salt and pepper

2 garlic cloves, finely chopped

2 fresh red chillies, deseeded and chopped

2 fresh green chillies, deseeded and chopped

400 g/14 oz dried penne

cook's tip

Do not overdrain pasta, as some of the starch that is left will help the sauce stick to the pasta. Alternatively, reserve 1–2 tablespoons of the pasta cooking water and stir it in before adding the sauce.

1 Melt the butter and 4 tablespoons of the olive oil in a large heavy-based saucepan. Add the mushrooms and cook over a medium heat, stirring occasionally, for 5 minutes. Stir in the flour and cook, stirring constantly, for 1 minute. Gradually stir in the Beef Stock and wine, bring to the boil, reduce the heat and simmer for 15 minutes. Add

the tomatoes, tomato purée, sugar and basil, season to taste with salt and pepper and simmer for a further 30 minutes.

2 Heat the remaining olive oil in a large frying pan. Add the garlic and chillies and cook, stirring constantly, for 5 minutes. Stir in the mushroom mixture, taste and

adjust the seasoning, if necessary, then simmer over a low heat for 20 minutes.

3 Meanwhile, bring a large heavy-based saucepan of lightly salted water to the boil. Add the pasta, return to the boil and cook for 8–10 minutes, or until tender but still firm to the bite.

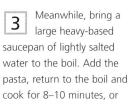

4 Drain the pasta and transfer to a warmed serving dish. Add the spicy mushroom sauce, toss well and serve immediately.

macaroni cheese special

serves 4   **prep: 10 mins**   **cook: 20 mins**

This version of the family favourite is always popular with children and makes the perfect weekend lunch dish.

INGREDIENTS

salt

225 g/8 oz dried short-cut macaroni

8 frankfurters

200 g/7 oz canned sweetcorn, drained

3 spring onions, thinly sliced

CHEESE SAUCE

40 g/1½ oz butter

40 g/1½ oz plain flour

425 ml/15 fl oz milk

salt and pepper

1 tbsp Dijon mustard

175 g/6 oz Cheddar cheese, grated

115 g/4 oz Gruyère cheese, grated

NUTRITIONAL INFORMATION

Calories	.898
Protein	.39g
Carbohydrate	.70g
Sugars	.12g
Fat	.53g
Saturates	.26g

variation

This dish would also work well with other dried short pasta shapes, such as rotelle, penne, fusilli bucati or even eliche (spirals).

1 Bring a large heavy-based saucepan of lightly salted water to the boil. Add the macaroni, return to the boil and cook for 8–10 minutes, or until tender but still firm to the bite. Meanwhile, cook the frankfurters in boiling water or in the microwave according to the packet instructions. Drain the macaroni and place in a large heatproof bowl, then cut the frankfurters into thick slices and stir them into the macaroni.

2 To make the sauce, melt the butter in a small saucepan. Add the flour and cook, stirring constantly, for 1 minute. Gradually stir in the milk, then bring to the boil, stirring constantly. Cook, stirring, for 1–2 minutes, or until thickened, then remove from the heat, season to taste with salt and pepper and stir in the mustard, Gruyère cheese, and 115 g/4 oz of the Cheddar cheese.

3 Stir the sweetcorn and spring onions into the macaroni, then fold in the sauce. Sprinkle the remaining grated Cheddar cheese evenly over the top and cook under a preheated hot grill for 2–3 minutes, or until the topping is golden and bubbling. Serve immediately.

pipe rigate with gorgonzola sauce

⏱ **cook: 12–15 mins**   ⏲ **prep: 5 mins**   **serves 4**

This is a very rich-tasting sauce, so a little of this dish goes a long way. It would make a good starter for an informal lunch party.

NUTRITIONAL INFORMATION	
Calories	770
Protein	. . . . .23g
Carbohydrate	. . . . .78g
Sugars	. . . . .4g
Fat	. . . . .43g
Saturates	. . . . .26g

INGREDIENTS

400 g/14 oz dried pipe rigate

25 g/1 oz unsalted butter

6 fresh sage leaves

200 g/7 oz Gorgonzola cheese, diced

175–225 ml/6–8 fl oz double cream or panna da cucina

2 tbsp dry vermouth

salt and pepper

cook's tip

Gorgonzola should be creamy coloured with pale green marbling and a pleasant aroma. Do not buy it if it is hard, discoloured or smelly.

1 Bring a large heavy-based saucepan of lightly salted water to the boil. Add the pasta, return to the boil and cook for 8–10 minutes, until tender but still firm to the bite.

2 Meanwhile, melt the butter in a separate heavy-based saucepan. Add the sage leaves and cook, stirring gently, for 1 minute. Remove and reserve the sage leaves. Add the cheese and cook, stirring constantly, over a low heat until it has melted. Gradually, stir in 175 ml/6 fl oz of the cream and the vermouth. Season to taste with salt and pepper and cook, stirring, until thickened. Add more cream if the sauce seems too thick.

3 Drain the pasta well and transfer to a warmed serving dish. Add the Gorgonzola sauce, toss well to mix and serve immediately, garnished with the reserved sage leaves.

fettuccine with ricotta

Very little cooking is involved in the preparation of this lovely, light pasta dish, so it makes an excellent choice for a light lunch in hot weather, served with mixed salad leaves.

INGREDIENTS

350 g/12 oz dried fettuccine

40 g/1½ oz unsalted butter

2 tbsp chopped fresh
flat-leaved parsley

115 g/4 oz ricotta cheese

115 g/4 oz ground almonds

150 ml/5 fl oz crème fraîche

2 tbsp extra virgin olive oil

125 ml/4 fl oz hot Chicken Stock
(see page 12)

pinch of freshly grated nutmeg

salt and pepper

1 tbsp pine kernels

fresh flat-leaved parsley leaves,
to garnish

NUTRITIONAL INFORMATION	
Calories	.730
Protein	.21g
Carbohydrate	.70g
Sugars	.5g
Fat	.43g
Saturates	.14g

variation

To give a sharp, piquant flavour to the sauce, add the finely grated rind and juice of ½ lemon with the ground almonds in Step 2.

cook's tip

It is important that you mix the ricotta, ground almonds and crème fraîche into a smooth paste before adding the oil in Step 2. Equally, don't add the stock until the oil has been completely absorbed.

1 Bring a large heavy-based saucepan of lightly salted water to the boil. Add the pasta, return to the boil and cook for 8–10 minutes, or until tender but still firm to the bite. Drain well and return to the saucepan. Add the butter and chopped parsley and toss thoroughly to coat.

2 Mix the ricotta, ground almonds and crème fraîche together in a bowl. Gradually stir in the olive oil, followed by the hot Chicken Stock. Season to taste with nutmeg and pepper.

3 Transfer the pasta to a warmed dish, pour over the sauce and toss. Sprinkle with pine kernels, garnish with parsley leaves and serve immediately.

pasta with pesto

serves 4   **prep: 15 mins**   **cook: 8–10 mins**

Home-made pesto is much more delicious than even good-quality, shop-bought brands and it makes a wonderful no-cook sauce for all types of freshly cooked pasta.

INGREDIENTS

175 g/6 oz fresh basil leaves

55 g/2 oz pine kernels

4 garlic cloves, roughly chopped

salt

225 g/8 oz freshly grated
Parmesan cheese

225 ml/8 fl oz extra virgin olive oil

450 g/1 lb dried spaghetti

fresh basil sprigs, to garnish (optional)

NUTRITIONAL INFORMATION	
Calories	1124
Protein	39g
Carbohydrate	87g
Sugars	4g
Fat	71g
Saturates	18g

cook's tip

If you want to make the pesto in advance, store it, covered with a thin layer of olive oil, in a screw-top jar in the refrigerator. It can be stored in the refrigerator for 3–4 days

1 Place the basil leaves, pine kernels and garlic in a large mortar and add a generous pinch of salt. Grind to a paste with a pestle. Gradually work in the Parmesan cheese until the mixture is smooth. Add the olive oil in a slow trickle, beating constantly with a wooden spoon, then reserve until required.

2 Bring a large heavy-based saucepan of lightly salted water to the boil. Add the pasta, return to the boil and cook for 8–10 minutes, or until tender but still firm to the bite.

3 Drain the pasta and reserve 1–2 tablespoons of the cooking water. If you like, thin the pesto slightly with the cooking water, then add to the pasta and toss well. Serve immediately, garnished with basil, if you like.

tagliatelle with walnuts

⏲ **cook: 8–10 mins**   ⏲ **prep: 10 mins**   **serves 4**

This unusual combination would make an intriguing starter for a dinner party, but is also great for a light lunch, if served with a crisp green salad and crusty bread.

NUTRITIONAL INFORMATION	
Calories	1124
Protein	. . . . .27g
Carbohydrate	. . . . .75g
Sugars	. . . . .9g
Fat	. . . . .82g
Saturates	. . . . .12g

INGREDIENTS

25 g/1 oz fresh white breadcrumbs

350 g/12 oz walnut pieces

2 garlic cloves, finely chopped

4 tbsp milk

4 tbsp olive oil

85 g/3 oz fromage frais or
cream cheese

150 ml/5 fl oz single cream

salt and pepper

350 g/12 oz dried tagliatelle

1 Place the breadcrumbs, walnuts, garlic, milk, olive oil and fromage frais in a large mortar and grind to a smooth paste. Alternatively, place the ingredients in a food processor and process until smooth. Stir in the cream to give a thick sauce consistency and season to taste with salt and pepper. Reserve.

2 Bring a large heavy-based saucepan of lightly salted water to the boil. Add the pasta, return to the boil and cook for 8–10 minutes, or until tender but still firm to the bite.

3 Drain the pasta and transfer to a warmed serving dish. Add the walnut sauce and toss thoroughly to coat. Serve immediately.

cook's tip

You may not need all of the walnut sauce as it is very rich. Store any leftover sauce in a screw-top jar in the refrigerator for up to 2 days.

saffron linguine

serves 4   **prep: 10 mins**   **cook: 12–15 mins**

Simple and colourful, this delightful dish is perfect for both family suppers and informal entertaining.

INGREDIENTS

350 g/12 oz dried linguine

pinch of saffron threads

2 tbsp water

140 g/5 oz ham, cut into strips

175 ml/6 fl oz double cream or panna da cucina

55 g/2 oz freshly grated Parmesan cheese

salt and pepper

2 egg yolks

NUTRITIONAL INFORMATION

Calories	.626
Protein	.25g
Carbohydrate	.66g
Sugars	.4g
Fat	.31g
Saturates	.17g

variation

Replace the ham with the same amount of pancetta or rindless, streaky bacon, cut into strips. For a special occasion, use Parma ham.

1 Bring a large heavy-based saucepan of lightly salted water to the boil. Add the pasta, return to the boil and cook for 8–10 minutes, or until tender but still firm to the bite.

2 Meanwhile, place the saffron in a separate heavy-based saucepan and add the water. Bring to the boil, then remove from the heat and leave to stand for 5 minutes.

3 Stir the ham, cream and grated Parmesan cheese into the saffron and return the saucepan to the heat. Season to taste with salt and pepper and heat through gently, stirring constantly, until simmering. Remove the saucepan from the heat and beat in the egg yolks. Drain the pasta and transfer to a warmed serving dish. Add the saffron sauce, toss well and serve immediately.

spaghetti olio e aglio

cook: 10 mins　　　　**prep: 5 mins**　　　　**serves 4**

This famous Roman recipe is probably the simplest pasta dish in the world – spaghetti with olive oil and garlic.

NUTRITIONAL INFORMATION

Calories 600

Protein 14g

Carbohydrate 84g

Sugars 4g

Fat 26g

Saturates 3g

INGREDIENTS

450 g/1 lb dried spaghetti

125 ml/4 fl oz extra virgin olive oil

3 garlic cloves, finely chopped

3 tbsp chopped fresh

flat-leaved parsley

salt and pepper

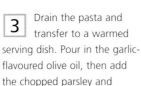

cook's tip

Cooked pasta gets cold quickly, so make sure that the serving dish is warmed thoroughly. As soon as the pasta is drained, transfer to the dish, pour over the garlic-flavoured olive oil, toss and serve.

1 Bring a large heavy-based saucepan of lightly salted water to the boil. Add the pasta, return to the boil and cook for 8–10 minutes, or until tender but still firm to the bite.

2 Meanwhile, heat the olive oil in a heavy-based frying pan. Add the garlic and a pinch of salt and cook over a low heat, stirring constantly, for 3–4 minutes, or until golden. Do not allow the garlic to brown or it will taste bitter. Remove the frying pan from the heat.

3 Drain the pasta and transfer to a warmed serving dish. Pour in the garlic-flavoured olive oil, then add the chopped parsley and season to taste with salt and pepper. Toss well and serve immediately.

tagliarini all'alfredo

This is a typical Italian first course – simple, but perfect. It also makes a quick and easy light meal.

INGREDIENTS

450 g/1 lb dried tagliarini

25 g/1 oz unsalted butter

200 ml/7 fl oz double cream or panna da cucina

55 g/2 oz freshly grated Parmesan cheese, plus extra to garnish

pinch of freshly grated nutmeg

salt and pepper

NUTRITIONAL INFORMATION

Calories	.720
Protein	.20g
Carbohydrate	.85g
Sugars	.5g
Fat	.36g
Saturates	.22g

variation

For a more substantial dish, cook 350 g/12 oz fresh or frozen peas in the butter for 3 minutes before adding the cream.

1 Bring a large heavy-based saucepan of lightly salted water to the boil. Add the pasta, return to the boil and cook for 8–10 minutes, or until tender but still firm to the bite.

2 Meanwhile, melt the butter in a separate heavy-based saucepan. Stir in 150 ml/5 fl oz of the cream, bring to the boil, then reduce the heat and simmer for 1 minute, until the mixture is slightly thickened.

3 Drain the pasta, then tip it into the butter and cream mixture and stir well to coat. Add the remaining cream and the grated Parmesan cheese. Season to taste with nutmeg, salt and pepper and stir. Serve immediately, garnished with extra grated Parmesan cheese.

linguine with spinach & anchovies

⏲ **cook: 15 mins**   ◔ **prep: 10 mins**   **serves 4**

Although it has a distinctive flavour, spinach is an astonishingly versatile vegetable, and is always delicious when paired with fish.

NUTRITIONAL INFORMATION

Calories 617

Protein 22g

Carbohydrate 78g

Sugars 7g

Fat 26g

Saturates 3g

INGREDIENTS

salt

400 g/14 oz dried linguine

900 g/2 lb spinach leaves, tough stalks removed

5 tbsp olive oil

3 tbsp pine kernels

2 garlic cloves, finely chopped

8 canned anchovy fillets, drained and chopped

cook's tip

Canned anchovy fillets can be quite salty, so to remove excess salt, place the anchovies in a small bowl and pour over enough milk to cover. Leave to soak for 10 minutes, then drain and pat dry with kitchen paper.

1 Bring a large heavy-based saucepan of lightly salted water to the boil. Add the pasta, return to the boil and cook for 8–10 minutes, or until tender but still firm to the bite.

2 Meanwhile, wash the spinach in several changes of water, then place in a large saucepan with only the water clinging to the leaves. Cover and cook over a high heat, shaking the saucepan occasionally, for 4–5 minutes, or until the spinach has wilted. Drain well.

3 Heat 4 tablespoons of the olive oil in a frying pan. Add the pine kernels and cook, stirring frequently, until golden. Remove from the frying pan with a slotted spoon and reserve. Reduce the heat, add the garlic to the frying pan and cook, stirring constantly, for 3–4 minutes, or until golden. Do not allow the garlic to brown or it will taste bitter.

4 Stir in the anchovies and spinach and cook, stirring constantly, for 2–3 minutes, then return the pine kernels to the frying pan. Drain the pasta, transfer to a warmed serving dish and add the remaining olive oil. Toss well, add the spinach and anchovy sauce, then toss again. Serve immediately.

meat & poultry

Both beef and chicken are indisputably the classic partners for pasta – think of Spaghetti &

Meatballs (see page 50), Lasagne al Forno (see page 54) or Creamy Chicken Ravioli (see

page 78). That said, you may be pleasantly surprised by some rather different recipes, such as

Pepperoni Pasta (see page 60), Chilli Pork with Tagliatelle (see page 62) and Bucatini with

Lamb & Yellow Pepper Sauce (see page 68). One of the great joys of pasta dishes is that there is

always at least one that is exactly right, whatever the occasion, season, level of culinary skill,

time available and extent of the budget. There are speedy midweek suppers to feed a hungry

family, robust baked dishes to take the chill off winter evenings, delicately flavoured filled pasta

that is ideal for entertaining, and hot and spicy mixtures to set the taste buds tingling.

Meat and poultry are combined with herbs, wine, olives, mushrooms, cheese, peppers and,

of course, tomatoes to make fabulous sauces and fillings for every kind of pasta, from curly

corkscrew fusilli to long strings of linguine and from bulging cannelloni tubes to the little

buttons of tortellini that are said to resemble Venus's navel. Whether you plan to make your

own dough for preparing ravioli or you have not planned at all and must ransack the refrigerator

and storecupboard for whatever is to hand, there is a perfect pasta dish to fit the bill.

classic tagliatelle bolognese

serves 4   prep: 15 mins   cook: 50–55 mins

Bologna is a close culinary rival to Rome and boasts some of the best restaurants in Italy. This signature dish is classically made with tagliatelle, rather than spaghetti.

INGREDIENTS

4 tbsp olive oil, plus extra for drizzling

85 g/3 oz pancetta or rindless streaky bacon, diced

1 onion, chopped

1 garlic clove, finely chopped

1 carrot, chopped

1 celery stick, chopped

225 g/8 oz fresh beef mince

115 g/4 oz chicken livers, chopped

2 tbsp passata

125 ml/4 fl oz dry white wine

225 ml/8 fl oz Beef Stock (see page 12) or water

1 tbsp chopped fresh oregano or marjoram

1 bay leaf

salt and pepper

450 g/1 lb dried tagliatelle

freshly grated Parmesan cheese, to serve

NUTRITIONAL INFORMATION

Calories	.700
Protein	.35g
Carbohydrate	.89g
Sugars	.8g
Fat	.24g
Saturates	.5g

---

variation

For a chunky sauce, replace the beef mince with the same amount of finely chopped fresh braising steak.

---

cook's tip

Cheap beef mince is a false economy, as it is very fatty. Look for lean beef mince or, better still, buy good-quality steak and mince it yourself.

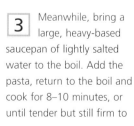

1 Heat the olive oil in a large, heavy-based saucepan. Add the diced pancetta and cook over a medium heat, stirring occasionally, for 3–5 minutes, or until turning brown. Add the onion, garlic, carrot and celery and cook, stirring occasionally, for a further 5 minutes.

2 Add the beef and cook over a high heat, breaking up the meat with a wooden spoon, for 5 minutes, or until browned. Stir in the chicken livers and cook, stirring occasionally, for a further 2–3 minutes. Add the passata, wine, Beef Stock, oregano and bay leaf and season to taste with salt and pepper. Bring to

the boil, reduce the heat, cover and simmer for 30–35 minutes.

3 Meanwhile, bring a large, heavy-based saucepan of lightly salted water to the boil. Add the pasta, return to the boil and cook for 8–10 minutes, or until tender but still firm to

the bite. Drain, transfer to a warmed serving dish, drizzle with a little olive oil and toss well. Remove and discard the bay leaf from the sauce, then pour it on to the pasta, toss again and serve with grated Parmesan cheese.

spaghetti & meatballs

cook: 45 mins

prep: 20 mins, plus 30 mins chilling

serves 6

NUTRITIONAL INFORMATION

Calories	.280
Protein	.18g
Carbohydrate	.40g
Sugars	.3g
Fat	.7g
Saturates	.1g

variation

For a spicier version, substitute a pinch of crushed, dried red chilli for the cayenne and stir ½ teaspoon crushed chilli into the sauce with the sugar.

A very popular dish with both children and adults, in which delicious, bite-sized meatballs are simmered in a rich tomato sauce and served on a bed of freshly cooked spaghetti.

INGREDIENTS

25 g/1 oz white bread, crusts removed and torn into pieces

2 tbsp milk

450 g/1 lb fresh beef mince

4 tbsp chopped fresh flat-leaved parsley

1 egg

pinch of cayenne pepper

salt and pepper

2 tbsp olive oil

150 ml/5 fl oz passata

200 g/7 oz canned chopped tomatoes

400 ml/14 fl oz Vegetable Stock (see page 12)

pinch of sugar

450 g/1 lb dried spaghetti

cook's tip

When forming the meat mixture into balls, dampen your hands slightly with a little cold water to help prevent the mixture from sticking.

1 Place the bread in a small bowl, add the milk and leave to soak. Meanwhile, place the beef in a large bowl and add half the parsley, the egg and the cayenne pepper. Season to taste with salt and pepper. Squeeze the excess moisture out of the bread and crumble it over the meat mixture. Mix well until smooth.

2 Form small pieces of the mixture into balls between the palms of your hands and place on a tray or board. Leave to chill in the refrigerator for 30 minutes.

3 Heat the olive oil in a large, heavy-based frying pan. Add the meatballs in batches, and cook, stirring and turning frequently, until

browned on all sides. Return earlier batches to the frying pan, add the passata, chopped tomatoes and their can juices, Vegetable Stock and sugar, then season to taste with salt and pepper. Bring to the boil, reduce the heat, cover and simmer for 25–30 minutes, or until the sauce is thickened and the meatballs are tender and cooked through.

4 Meanwhile, bring a large, heavy-based saucepan of lightly salted water to the boil. Add the pasta, return to the boil and cook for 8–10 minutes, or until tender but still firm to the bite. Drain and transfer to a warmed serving dish. Pour the sauce over the pasta and toss lightly. Sprinkle with the remaining parsley and serve immediately.

pasta soufflé

serves 4   **prep: 20 mins**   **cook: 1 hr 15 mins**

A variation on the classic pasta bolognese, this is an economical dish that is perfect for family meals and informal entertaining.

INGREDIENTS

2 tbsp olive oil

1 large onion, chopped

225 g/8 oz fresh beef mince

1 garlic clove, finely chopped

400 g/14 oz canned chopped tomatoes

1 tbsp tomato purée

salt and pepper

175 g/6 oz dried elbow macaroni

butter, for greasing

3 eggs, separated

40 g/1½ oz freshly grated Parmesan cheese, plus extra for sprinkling

---

NUTRITIONAL INFORMATION

Calories 427

Protein 28g

Carbohydrate 42g

Sugars 8g

Fat 18g

Saturates 6g

---

variation

Substitute the dried elbow macaroni with other dried small pasta shapes, such as penne, conchiglie or rigatoni.

---

cook's tip

Parmesan cheese is an Italian hard cheese made from skimmed milk. If possible, try to buy fresh Parmesan cheese in a block and grate it yourself as its flavour is far superior to that of the dried cheese.

1 Preheat the oven to 190°C/375°F/Gas Mark 5. Heat the olive oil in a large, heavy-based frying pan. Add the onion and cook over a low heat, stirring occasionally, for 5 minutes, or until softened. Add the beef and cook, breaking up the meat with a wooden spoon, until browned. Stir in the garlic, tomatoes and their can juices and tomato purée, then season to taste with salt and pepper. Bring to the boil, reduce the heat and simmer for 20 minutes, then remove the frying pan from the heat and leave to cool slightly.

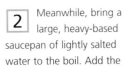

2 Meanwhile, bring a large, heavy-based saucepan of lightly salted water to the boil. Add the pasta, return to the boil and cook for 8–10 minutes, or until tender but still firm to the bite. Drain and reserve.

3 Lightly grease a 1.2-litre/ 2-pint soufflé dish with butter. Beat the egg yolks and add them to the meat sauce, then stir in the pasta. Whisk the egg whites until stiff peaks form, then fold into the sauce.

Spoon the mixture into the dish, sprinkle with the grated Parmesan cheese and bake in the preheated oven for 45 minutes, or until well risen and golden brown. Sprinkle with extra grated Parmesan cheese and serve immediately.

lasagne al forno

serves 4   **prep: 15 mins**   **cook: 1 hr 15 mins**

Layers of pasta, meat sauce and lasagne, all covered with a rich cheese sauce, makes a tasty and substantial family supper.

INGREDIENTS

2 tbsp olive oil

55 g/2 oz pancetta or rindless streaky bacon, chopped

1 onion, chopped

1 garlic clove, finely chopped

225 g/8 oz fresh beef mince

2 celery sticks, chopped

2 carrots, chopped

salt and pepper

pinch of sugar

½ tsp dried oregano

400 g/14 oz canned chopped tomatoes

225 g/8 oz dried no-pre-cook lasagne

115 g/4 oz freshly grated Parmesan cheese, plus extra for sprinkling

CHEESE SAUCE

2 tsp Dijon mustard

70 g/2½ oz Cheddar cheese, grated

70 g/2½ oz Gruyère cheese, grated

300 ml/10 fl oz hot Béchamel Sauce (see page 12)

NUTRITIONAL INFORMATION

Calories 800

Protein 46g

Carbohydrate 61g

Sugars 15g

Fat 42g

Saturates 22g

variation

Substitute the Gruyère cheese with another good melting cheese, such as Emmenthal, if you prefer.

cook's tip

You can use either plain or egg lasagne sheets in this dish. They are available in three colours: plain lasagne is yellow, spinach lasagne or lasagne verde is green, while wholewheat lasagne is brown.

1 Preheat the oven to 190°C/375°F/Gas Mark 5. Heat the olive oil in a large, heavy-based saucepan. Add the pancetta and cook over a medium heat, stirring occasionally, for 3 minutes, or until the fat begins to run. Add the onion and garlic and cook, stirring occasionally, for 5 minutes, or until softened.

2 Add the beef and cook, breaking it up with a wooden spoon, until browned all over. Stir in the celery and carrot and cook for 5 minutes. Season to taste with salt and pepper. Add the sugar, oregano and tomatoes and their can juices. Bring to the boil, reduce the heat and simmer for 30 minutes.

3 Meanwhile, to make the cheese sauce, stir the mustard and both cheeses into the hot Béchamel Sauce.

4 In a large, rectangular ovenproof dish, make alternate layers of meat sauce, lasagne and Parmesan cheese. Pour the cheese sauce over the layers, covering them

completely, and sprinkle with Parmesan cheese. Bake in the preheated oven for 30 minutes, or until golden brown and bubbling. Serve immediately.

mixed meat lasagne

serves 6   **prep: 20 mins**   **cook: 1 hr 35 mins**

*This is a wonderful dish for an informal supper party.
Serve with a crisp green salad, some crusty Italian bread and,
perhaps, a bottle or two of red wine.*

INGREDIENTS

1 onion, chopped

1 carrot, chopped

1 celery stick, chopped

85 g/3 oz pancetta or rindless
streaky bacon, chopped

175 g/6 oz fresh beef mince

175 g/6 oz fresh pork mince

3 tbsp olive oil

100 ml/3½ fl oz red wine

150 ml/5 fl oz Beef Stock (see page 12)

1 tbsp tomato purée

1 bay leaf

1 clove

salt and pepper

150 ml/5 fl oz milk

55 g/2 oz butter, diced, plus extra
for greasing

400 g/14 oz dried no-pre-cook
lasagne verde

600 ml/1 pint Béchamel Sauce
(see page 12)

140 g/5 oz freshly grated
Parmesan cheese

140 g/5 oz mozzarella cheese, diced

variation

For a lighter dish, substitute fresh
chicken mince for the beef and pork
mince and Chicken Stock for the Beef
Stock (see page 12).

cook's tip

Bay leaves are available in
both fresh and dried forms.
Always use sparingly as
their strong flavour can be
overwhelming. They are
best used in robust, well-
flavoured dishes.

1 Mix the chopped onion, carrot, celery, pancetta, beef and pork together in a large bowl. Heat the olive oil in a large, heavy-based frying pan, add the meat mixture and cook over a medium heat, breaking up the meat with a wooden spoon, until it is browned all over. Pour in the red wine, then bring to the boil and cook until reduced.

Pour in 125 ml/4 fl oz of the Beef Stock, bring to the boil and cook until reduced.

2 Mix the tomato purée and remaining Beef Stock together in a small bowl, then add to the frying pan with the bay leaf and clove. Season to taste with salt and pepper and pour in the milk. Cover and simmer for 1 hour.

3 Preheat the oven to 200°C/400°F/Gas Mark 6. Remove and discard the bay leaf and the clove from the meat sauce. Lightly grease a large, ovenproof dish with butter. Make alternate layers of lasagne, meat sauce, Béchamel Sauce and Parmesan and mozzarella cheese in the dish, ending with Béchamel Sauce sprinkled with cheese.

4 Dot the top of the lasagne with butter and bake in the preheated oven for 25 minutes, or until golden brown. Serve immediately.

sicilian linguine

cook: 1 hr 15 mins   **prep: 20 mins**   **serves 4**

NUTRITIONAL INFORMATION

Calories 680

Protein 38g

Carbohydrate . . . . :.45g

Sugars 12g

Fat 40g

Saturates 11g

variation

Other types of long pasta also work well in this dish, such as spaghetti. Replace the red pepper with a yellow pepper, if you like.

This delicious classic dish of aubergines, tomatoes, meat and olives is perfect for both a family midweek supper or a special occasion main course. Serve with a fresh green salad.

INGREDIENTS

125 ml/4 fl oz olive oil

2 aubergines, sliced

350 g/12 oz fresh beef mince

1 onion, chopped

2 garlic cloves, finely chopped

2 tbsp tomato purée

400 g/14 oz canned chopped tomatoes

1 tsp Worcestershire sauce

1 tbsp chopped fresh
flat-leaved parsley

salt and pepper

55 g/2 oz stoned black olives, sliced

1 red pepper, deseeded and chopped

175 g/6 oz dried linguine

115 g/4 oz freshly grated
Parmesan cheese

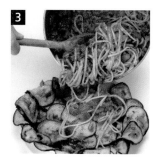

cook's tip

After frying the aubergines, leave them to drain on kitchen paper for a few minutes because they tend to absorb quite a lot of the oil during the cooking and may make the finished dish quite oily.

1 Preheat the oven to 200°C/400°F/Gas Mark 6. Brush a 20-cm/8-inch loose-bottomed round cake tin with oil and line the base with baking paper. Heat half the oil in a frying pan. Add the aubergines in batches, and fry until lightly browned on both sides. Add more oil, as required. Drain the aubergines on kitchen paper, then arrange in overlapping slices to cover the base and sides of the cake tin, reserving a few slices.

2 Heat the remaining olive oil in a large saucepan and add the beef, onion and garlic. Cook over a medium heat, breaking up the meat with a wooden spoon, until browned all over. Add the tomato purée, tomatoes and their can juices, Worcestershire sauce and parsley. Season to taste with salt and pepper and simmer for 10 minutes. Add the olives and red pepper and cook for a further 10 minutes.

3 Meanwhile, bring a saucepan of lightly salted water to the boil. Add the pasta, return to the boil and cook for 8–10 minutes, or until tender but still firm to the bite. Drain and transfer to a bowl. Add the meat sauce and cheese and toss, then spoon into the cake tin, press down and cover with the remaining aubergine slices. Bake in the oven for 40 minutes. Leave for 5 minutes, then loosen around the edges and invert on to a plate. Remove and discard the baking paper and serve.

pepperoni pasta

serves 4   **prep: 10 mins**   **cook: 20 mins**

Quick and easy, colourful and scrumptious – what more could a hungry family want for a midweek supper?

INGREDIENTS

3 tbsp olive oil	1 tsp paprika
1 onion, chopped	225 g/8 oz pepperoni sausage, sliced
1 red pepper, deseeded and diced	2 tbsp chopped fresh flat-leaved
1 orange pepper, deseeded and diced	parsley, plus extra to garnish
800 g/1 lb 12 oz canned	salt and pepper
chopped tomatoes	450 g/1 lb dried garganelli
1 tbsp sun-dried tomato paste	mixed salad leaves, to serve

variation

If you cannot find garganelli pasta, then use penne or another pasta shape, such as fusilli bucati or farfalle.

cook's tip

Pepperoni is a hotly spiced Italian sausage made from pork and beef and is flavoured with fennel. You could substitute other spicy sausages, such as kabanos or chorizo, if you like.

1 Heat 2 tablespoons of the olive oil in a large heavy-based frying pan. Add the onion and cook over a low heat, stirring occasionally, for 5 minutes, or until softened. Add the red and orange peppers, tomatoes and their can juices, sun-dried tomato paste and paprika and bring to the boil.

2 Add the pepperoni and parsley and season to taste with salt and pepper. Stir well, bring to the boil, then reduce the heat and simmer for 10–15 minutes.

3 Meanwhile, bring a large heavy-based saucepan of lightly salted water to the boil. Add the

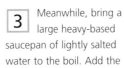

pasta, return to the boil and cook for 8–10 minutes, or until tender but still firm to the bite. Drain well and transfer to a warmed serving dish. Add the remaining olive oil and toss. Add the sauce and toss again. Sprinkle with parsley and serve immediately with mixed salad leaves.

chilli pork with tagliatelle

cook: 10 mins   **prep: 10 mins**   **serves 4**

NUTRITIONAL INFORMATION

Calories	755
Protein	. . . . .37g
Carbohydrate	. . . . .92g
Sugars	. . . . .9g
Fat	. . . . .29g
Saturates	. . . . .13g

variation

Substitute the pork fillet with the same amount of skinless, boneless chicken breast, cut into thin strips. Make sure it is thoroughly cooked before serving.

East meets West in this spicy dish. However, if you want a more authentically Asian-style meal, you could serve the sauce with egg or cellophane noodles.

INGREDIENTS

450 g/1 lb dried tagliatelle

3 tbsp groundnut oil

350 g/12 oz pork fillet, cut into thin strips

1 garlic clove, finely chopped

1 bunch of spring onions, sliced

2.5-cm/1-inch piece of fresh root ginger, grated

2 fresh bird's eye chillies, deseeded and finely chopped

1 red pepper, deseeded and cut into thin batons

1 yellow pepper, deseeded and cut into thin batons

3 courgettes, cut into thin batons

2 tbsp finely chopped peanuts

1 tsp ground cinnamon

1 tbsp oyster sauce

55 g/2 oz creamed coconut, grated

salt and pepper

2 tbsp chopped fresh coriander, to garnish

cook's tip

Bird's eye chillies, popular in Thai cuisine, are small and pointed and may be red, white, orange or green. They are invariably very hot. If you prefer a milder flavour, use serrano or Anaheim chillies.

1 Bring a large heavy-based saucepan of lightly salted water to the boil. Add the pasta, return to the boil and cook for 8–10 minutes, or until tender but still firm to the bite.

2 Meanwhile, heat the groundnut oil in a preheated wok or large frying pan. Add the pork and stir-fry for 5 minutes. Add the garlic, spring onions, ginger and bird's eye chillies and stir-fry for 2 minutes.

3 Add the red and yellow peppers and the courgettes and stir-fry for 1 minute. Add the peanuts, cinnamon, oyster sauce and creamed coconut and stir-fry for a further 1 minute. Season to taste with salt and pepper. Drain the pasta and transfer to a serving dish. Top with the chilli pork, sprinkle with the chopped coriander and serve.

pork & pasta bake

serves 4   **prep: 20 mins** ⟳   **cook: 1 hr 15 mins** ⟳

*This warm and filling dish is virtually a meal in itself –
perfect for a cold winter's evening. Serve it with mixed
green and red salad leaves, if you like.*

INGREDIENTS

2 tbsp olive oil

1 onion, chopped

1 garlic clove, finely chopped

2 carrots, diced

55 g/2 oz pancetta or rindless
streaky bacon, chopped

115 g/4 oz mushrooms, chopped

450 g/1 lb fresh pork mince

125 ml/4 fl oz dry white wine

4 tbsp passata

200 g/7 oz canned chopped tomatoes

2 tsp chopped fresh sage or ½ tsp
dried sage

salt and pepper

225 g/8 oz dried elecoidali

140 g/5 oz mozzarella cheese, diced

4 tbsp freshly grated Parmesan cheese

300 ml/10 fl oz hot Béchamel Sauce

(see page 12)

variation

Substitute the passata with the same
amount of tomato purée and the
canned tomatoes with fresh plum
tomatoes, peeled and finely chopped.

cook's tip

When cooking with olive oil,
try not to use extra virgin olive
oil as the flavour will be lost
during cooking. Olive oil is best
stored in a cool place, out of
direct sunlight. Do not store in
the refrigerator.

1 Preheat the oven to
200°C/400°F/Gas
Mark 6. Heat the olive oil in a
large heavy-based frying pan.
Add the onion, garlic and
carrots and cook over a low
heat, stirring occasionally, for
5 minutes, or until the
onion has softened. Add
the pancetta and cook for
5 minutes. Add the chopped
mushrooms and cook, stirring

occasionally, for a further
2 minutes. Add the pork and
cook, breaking it up with a
wooden spoon, until the meat
is browned all over. Stir in the
wine, passata, chopped
tomatoes and their can juices
and sage. Season to taste
with salt and pepper, bring
to the boil, then cover and
simmer over a low heat for
25–30 minutes.

2 Meanwhile, bring a
large heavy-based
saucepan of lightly salted
water to the boil. Add the
pasta, return to the boil and
cook for 8–10 minutes, or
until tender but still firm to
the bite.

3 Spoon the pork mixture
into a large ovenproof
dish. Stir the mozzarella and

half the Parmesan cheese into
the Béchamel Sauce. Drain the
pasta and stir the sauce into it,
then spoon it over the pork
mixture. Sprinkle with the
remaining Parmesan cheese
and bake in the oven for
25–30 minutes, or until golden
brown. Serve immediately.

pasticcio

 **cook: 1 hr 40 mins**   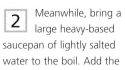 **prep: 15 mins**   **serves 4**

Not every pasta recipe has its origins in Italy. This is a traditional Greek bake made with lamb. It is delicious served hot or cold.

INGREDIENTS

1 tbsp olive oil	salt and pepper
1 onion, chopped	1 tsp ground cinnamon
2 garlic cloves, finely chopped	115 g/4 oz dried short-cut macaroni
450 g/1 lb fresh lamb mince	2 beef tomatoes, sliced
2 tbsp tomato purée	300 ml/10 fl oz Greek yogurt
2 tbsp plain flour	2 eggs, lightly beaten
300 ml/10 fl oz Chicken Stock	
(see page 12)	

variation

Pasticcio is also delicious made with fresh turkey or chicken mince. Replace the Greek yogurt with the same amount of natural yogurt, if you like.

cook's tip

If the meat sauce is too runny, then add an extra tablespoon of flour to the sauce and cook, stirring constantly, until the sauce has thickened slightly.

1 Preheat the oven to 190°C/375°F/Gas Mark 5. Heat the olive oil in a large heavy-based frying pan. Add the onion and garlic and cook over a low heat, stirring occasionally, for 5 minutes, or until softened. Add the lamb and cook, breaking it up with a wooden spoon, until browned all over. Add the tomato purée and sprinkle in the flour. Cook, stirring, for 1 minute, then stir in the Chicken Stock. Season to taste with salt and pepper and stir in the cinnamon. Bring to the boil, reduce the heat, cover and cook for 25 minutes.

2 Meanwhile, bring a large heavy-based saucepan of lightly salted water to the boil. Add the pasta, return to the boil and cook for 8–10 minutes, or until tender but still firm to the bite.

3 Spoon the lamb mixture into a large ovenproof dish and arrange the tomato slices on top. Drain the pasta and transfer to a bowl. Add the yogurt and eggs and mix well. Spoon the pasta mixture on top of the lamb and bake in the preheated oven for 1 hour. Serve immediately.

bucatini with lamb & yellow pepper sauce

serves 4   **prep: 10 mins**   **cook: 1 hr**

This regional speciality is traditionally served with square-shaped macaroni, but this is not widely available. That said, you may find it in an Italian delicatessen. This recipe uses bucatini instead.

INGREDIENTS

4 tbsp olive oil

280 g/10 oz boneless lamb, cubed

1 garlic clove, finely chopped

1 bay leaf

225 ml/8 fl oz dry white wine

salt and pepper

2 large yellow peppers, deseeded and diced

4 tomatoes, peeled and chopped

250 g/9 oz dried bucatini

NUTRITIONAL INFORMATION

Calories 704

Protein 31g

Carbohydrate 98g

Sugars 10g

Fat 20g

Saturates 5g

cook's tip

Bucatini is a long, thin, hollow pasta. If you are unable to find bucatini, then substitute spaghetti or another similar type of long pasta instead.

1 Heat half the olive oil in a large heavy-based frying pan. Add the cubes of lamb and cook over a medium heat, stirring frequently, until browned on all sides. Add the garlic and cook for a further 1 minute. Add the bay leaf, pour in the wine and season to taste with salt and pepper. Bring to the boil and cook for 5 minutes, or until reduced.

2 Stir in the remaining oil, peppers and tomatoes. Reduce the heat, cover and simmer, stirring occasionally, for 45 minutes.

3 Meanwhile, bring a large heavy-based saucepan of lightly salted water to the boil. Add the pasta, return to the boil and cook for 8–10 minutes, or until tender but still firm to the bite. Drain and transfer to a warmed serving dish. Remove and discard the bay leaf from the lamb sauce and spoon the sauce on to the pasta. Toss well and serve immediately.

spaghetti with parsley chicken

cook: 15 mins   **prep: 15 mins**   **serves 4**

Lemon, ginger and fresh flat-leaved parsley give an extra lift to the chicken and pasta in this lovely summery dish. Use fresh spaghetti instead of the dried, if you prefer.

NUTRITIONAL INFORMATION

Calories	.430
Protein	.21g
Carbohydrate	.52g
Sugars	.7g
Fat	.17g
Saturates	.8g

INGREDIENTS

1 tbsp olive oil

thinly pared rind of 1 lemon, cut into julienne strips

1 tsp finely chopped fresh root ginger

1 tsp sugar

salt

225 ml/8 fl oz Chicken Stock (see page 12)

250 g/9 oz dried spaghetti

55 g/2 oz butter

225 g/8 oz skinless, boneless chicken breasts, diced

1 red onion, finely chopped

leaves from 2 bunches of flat-leaved parsley

cook's tip

Use an unwaxed lemon, if possible, and wash before paring the rind. If only waxed lemons are available – or you are not sure – scrub with a vegetable brush.

1 Heat the olive oil in a heavy-based saucepan. Add the lemon rind and cook over a low heat, stirring frequently, for 5 minutes. Stir in the ginger and sugar, season to taste with salt and cook, stirring constantly, for a further 2 minutes. Pour in the Chicken Stock, bring to the boil, then cook for 5 minutes, or until the liquid has reduced by half.

2 Meanwhile, bring a large heavy-based saucepan of lightly salted water to the boil. Add the pasta, return to the boil and cook for 8–10 minutes, or until tender but still firm to the bite.

3 Meanwhile, melt half the butter in a frying pan. Add the chicken and onion and cook, stirring frequently, for 5 minutes, or until the chicken is light brown all over. Stir in the lemon and ginger mixture and cook for 1 minute. Stir in the parsley leaves and cook, stirring constantly, for a further 3 minutes.

4  Drain the pasta and transfer to a warmed serving dish, then add the remaining butter and toss well. Add the chicken sauce, toss again and serve.

cannelloni with ham & ricotta

serves 4   prep: 10 mins   cook: 1 hr 5 mins

*More delicately flavoured than the usual beef-filled cannelloni,
this is still a substantial dish for a family supper.*

INGREDIENTS

2 tbsp olive oil

2 onions, chopped

2 garlic cloves, finely chopped

1 tbsp shredded fresh basil

800 g/1 lb 12 oz canned
chopped tomatoes

1 tbsp tomato purée

salt and pepper

350 g/12 oz cannelloni tubes

butter, for greasing

225 g/8 oz ricotta cheese

115 g/4 oz cooked ham, diced

1 egg

55 g/2 oz freshly grated
pecorino cheese

variation

Substitute the pecorino cheese with
the same amount of freshly grated
Parmesan cheese, if you prefer.

cook's tip

Make sure that the cooked
cannelloni tubes are dry
before filling as they may go
soggy during cooking. Pat dry
thoroughly with kitchen paper
before filling with the ham
and ricotta mixture.

 1 Preheat the oven to 180°C/350°F/Gas Mark 4. Heat the olive oil in a large heavy-based frying pan. Add the onions and garlic and cook over a low heat, stirring occasionally, for 5 minutes, or until the onion is softened. Add the basil, chopped tomatoes and their can juices and tomato purée and season to taste with salt and pepper.

Reduce the heat and simmer for 30 minutes, or until thickened.

2 Meanwhile, bring a large heavy-based saucepan of lightly salted water to the boil. Add the cannelloni tubes, return to the boil and cook for 8–10 minutes, or until tender but still firm to the bite. Using

a slotted spoon, transfer the cannelloni tubes to a large plate and pat dry with kitchen paper.

3 Grease a large, shallow ovenproof dish with butter. Mix the ricotta, ham and egg together in a bowl and season to taste with salt and pepper. Using a teaspoon, fill the cannelloni tubes with

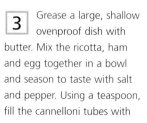

the ricotta mixture and place in a single layer in the dish. Pour the tomato sauce over the cannelloni and sprinkle with the grated pecorino cheese. Bake in the preheated oven for 30 minutes, or until golden brown. Serve immediately.

linguine with bacon & olives

⏲ **cook: 10 mins**　　　　⏱ **prep: 10 mins**　　　　**serves 4**

variation

If you like, use a mixture of wild mushrooms for extra flavour and substitute prosciutto for the bacon.

This wonderfully speedy dish, made mainly from storecupboard ingredients, tastes fabulous and is great for feeding unexpected guests. Serve with salad and bread for a filling supper.

INGREDIENTS

3 tbsp olive oil

2 onions, thinly sliced

2 garlic cloves, finely chopped

175 g/6 oz rindless lean bacon, diced

225 g/8 oz mushrooms, sliced

5 canned anchovy fillets, drained

6 black olives, stoned and halved

salt and pepper

450 g/1 lb dried linguine

25 g/1 oz freshly grated Parmesan cheese

cook's tip

You can buy olives that have been stoned already in jars or cans from most supermarkets, although try not to buy ones stored in brine as they may make the dish too salty.

1 Heat the olive oil in a large frying pan. Add the onions, garlic and bacon and cook over a low heat, stirring occasionally, until the onions are softened. Stir in the mushrooms, anchovies and olives, then season to taste with salt, if necessary, and pepper. Simmer for 5 minutes.

2 Meanwhile, bring a large heavy-based saucepan of lightly salted water to the boil. Add the pasta, return to the boil and cook for 8–10 minutes, or until tender but still firm to the bite.

3 Drain the pasta and transfer to a warmed serving dish. Spoon the sauce on top, toss lightly and sprinkle with the Parmesan cheese. Serve immediately.

chicken lasagne

*This lighter variation of the classic Lasagne al Forno
(see page 54) is especially popular with children.*

INGREDIENTS

2 tbsp olive oil

900 g/2 lb fresh chicken mince

1 garlic clove, finely chopped

4 carrots, chopped

4 leeks, sliced

450 ml/16 fl oz Chicken Stock

(see page 12)

2 tbsp tomato purée

salt and pepper

115 g/4 oz Cheddar cheese, grated

1 tsp Dijon mustard

600 ml/1 pint hot Béchamel Sauce

(see page 12)

115 g/4 oz dried no-pre-cook lasagne

NUTRITIONAL INFORMATION

Calories 570

Protein 46g

Carbohydrate 37g

Sugars 13g

Fat 27g

Saturates 13g

variation

Substitute the fresh chicken mince with
the same amount of turkey mince and
add 175 g/6 oz chopped chicken livers,
if you like.

cook's tip

When frying the chicken
mince, keep stirring it with a
wooden spoon to break up any
lumps and to seal in the
flavour. Make sure it is
browned all over before adding
the rest of the ingredients.

1 Preheat the oven to
190°C/ 375°F/Gas
Mark 5. Heat the oil in a
heavy-based saucepan. Add
the chicken and cook over a
medium heat, breaking it up
with a wooden spoon, for
5 minutes, or until it is
browned all over. Add the
garlic, carrots and leeks and
cook, stirring occasionally for
5 minutes.

2 Stir in the Chicken
Stock and tomato purée
and season to taste with salt
and pepper. Bring to the boil,
reduce the heat, cover and
simmer for 30 minutes.

3 Whisk half the Cheddar
cheese and the mustard
into the hot Béchamel Sauce.
In a large ovenproof dish,
make alternate layers of the

chicken mixture, lasagne and
cheese sauce, ending with a
layer of cheese sauce. Sprinkle
with the remaining Cheddar
cheese and bake in the
preheated oven for 1 hour,
or until golden brown and
bubbling. Serve immediately.

chicken & wild mushroom cannelloni

serves 4   **prep: 15 mins**   **cook: 1 hr 45 mins**

Cannelloni tubes filled with a delicious mix of wild mushrooms, chicken and prosciutto make a wonderful dinner party main course. Serve with a crisp green salad, if you like.

INGREDIENTS

butter, for greasing	1 tbsp shredded fresh basil leaves
2 tbsp olive oil	2 tbsp tomato purée
2 garlic cloves, crushed	salt and pepper
1 large onion, finely chopped	10–12 cannelloni tubes
225 g/8 oz wild mushrooms, sliced	600 ml/1 pint Béchamel Sauce
350 g/12 oz fresh chicken mince	(see page 12)
115 g/4 oz prosciutto, diced	85 g/3 oz freshly grated
150 ml/5 fl oz Marsala wine	Parmesan cheese
200 g/7 oz canned chopped tomatoes	

NUTRITIONAL INFORMATION

Calories	.830
Protein	.48g
Carbohydrate	.62g
Sugars	.17g
Fat	.36g
Saturates	.17g

variation

If you like, replace the Marsala wine with the same amount of brandy and substitute the canned tomatoes with the same amount of fresh tomatoes.

cook's tip

You can use any combination of wild mushrooms. For extra flavour, add 25 g/1 oz dried porcini, soaked in hot water for 30 minutes.

1 Preheat the oven to 190°C/375°F/Gas Mark 5. Lightly grease a large ovenproof dish. Heat the olive oil in a heavy-based frying pan. Add the garlic, onion and mushrooms and cook over a low heat, stirring frequently, for 8–10 minutes. Add the chicken mince and prosciutto and cook, stirring frequently, for 12 minutes, or until browned all over. Stir in the Marsala, tomatoes and their can juices, basil and tomato purée and cook for 4 minutes. Season to taste with salt and pepper, then cover and simmer for 30 minutes. Uncover, stir and simmer for 15 minutes.

2 Meanwhile, bring a large heavy-based saucepan of lightly salted water to the boil. Add the pasta, return to the boil and cook for 8–10 minutes, or until tender but still firm to the bite. Using a slotted spoon, transfer the cannelloni tubes to a plate and pat dry with kitchen paper.

3 Using a teaspoon, fill the cannelloni tubes with the chicken and mushroom mixture. Transfer them to the dish. Pour the Béchamel Sauce over them to cover completely and sprinkle with the grated Parmesan cheese.

4 Bake in the preheated oven for 30 minutes, or until golden brown and bubbling. Serve immediately.

creamy chicken ravioli

cook: 15 mins

prep: 30 mins, plus 1 hr resting

serves 4

Although it takes some time to prepare, this dish is extremely easy, but is sure to impress.

NUTRITIONAL INFORMATION	
Calories	.745
Protein	.30g
Carbohydrate	.43g
Sugars	.4g
Fat	.53g
Saturates	.29g

variation

If chestnut mushrooms are unavailable, use the same amount of wild mushrooms, such as chanterelle or field. Alternatively, use shiitake mushrooms.

INGREDIENTS

115 g/4 oz cooked skinless, boneless chicken breast, roughly chopped (see Cook's Tip)

55 g/2 oz cooked spinach

55 g/2 oz prosciutto, roughly chopped

1 shallot, roughly chopped

6 tbsp freshly grated pecorino cheese

pinch of freshly grated nutmeg

2 eggs, lightly beaten

salt and pepper

1 quantity Basic Pasta Dough (see page 13)

plain white flour, for dusting

300 ml/10 fl oz double cream or panna da cucina

2 garlic cloves, finely chopped

115 g/4 oz chestnut mushrooms, thinly sliced

2 tbsp shredded fresh basil

fresh basil sprigs, to garnish

cook's tip

To cook the chicken breast, place it in a saucepan with 1 tablespoon lemon juice and just enough water to cover. Season to taste with salt and pepper and poach gently for 10 minutes, or until cooked.

1 Place the chicken, spinach, prosciutto and shallot in a food processor and process until chopped and blended. Transfer to a bowl, stir in 2 tablespoons of the cheese, the nutmeg and half the egg. Season with salt and pepper.

2 Halve the Pasta Dough. Wrap one piece in clingfilm and thinly roll out the other on a lightly floured work surface. Cover with a tea towel and roll out the second piece of dough. Place small mounds of the filling in rows 4 cm/1½ inches apart on one sheet of dough and brush the spaces in between with beaten egg. Lift the second piece of dough to fit on top. Press down firmly between the mounds of filling, pushing out any air. Cut into squares and place on a floured tea towel. Leave the ravioli to rest for 1 hour.

3 Bring a large saucepan of lightly salted water to the boil. Add the ravioli in batches, return to the boil and cook for 5 minutes. Remove with a slotted spoon and drain on kitchen paper, then transfer to a warmed dish.

4 Meanwhile, pour the cream into a frying pan, add the garlic and bring to the boil. Simmer for 1 minute, then add the mushrooms and 2 tablespoons of the remaining cheese. Season to taste and simmer for 3 minutes. Stir in the basil, then pour the sauce over the ravioli. Sprinkle with the remaining cheese, garnish with basil sprigs and serve.

chicken & bacon tortellini

Serve these little stuffed pasta bites plain, sprinkled with Parmesan, or with a sauce of your choice, such as Neapolitan (see page 134), wild mushrooms (see page 163) or pesto (see page 40).

INGREDIENTS

15 g/½ oz butter

115 g/4 oz skinless, boneless chicken breast, diced

115 g/4 oz pork fillet, diced

115 g/4 oz pancetta or rindless streaky bacon, diced

55 g/2 oz mortadella sausage, roughly chopped

115 g/4 oz freshly grated Parmesan cheese, plus extra for sprinkling

2 eggs, lightly beaten

pinch of ground mixed spice

salt and pepper

2 quantities Basic Pasta Dough (see page 13)

plain flour, for dusting

NUTRITIONAL INFORMATION

Calories 575

Protein 34g

Carbohydrate 51g

Sugars 1g

Fat 28g

Saturates 11g

variation

If you like, serve the tortellini with a side dish of chopped fresh tomatoes, garnished with fresh basil sprigs.

cook's tip

When working with fresh pasta dough, always make sure that any dough you are not using is covered or wrapped in clingfilm to prevent it drying out.

1 Melt the butter in a large heavy-based frying pan. Add the chicken, pork and pancetta and cook over a medium heat, stirring frequently, until lightly browned all over. Remove from the frying pan and leave to cool slightly, then transfer to a food processor. Add the mortadella sausage, Parmesan cheese and half the eggs and process until chopped and blended. Scrape the mixture into a large bowl and season to taste with the mixed spice, salt and pepper.

2 Halve the Pasta Dough. Wrap one piece in clingfilm and roll out the other on a lightly floured work surface or chopping board to 1 cm/ ½ inch thick. Cover with a tea towel and roll out the second piece of dough. Stamp out rounds with a 5-cm/2-inch pastry cutter.

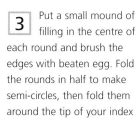

3 Put a small mound of filling in the centre of each round and brush the edges with beaten egg. Fold the rounds in half to make semi-circles, then fold them around the tip of your index finger and press the ends together. Bring a large pan of lightly salted water to the boil. Add the tortellini in batches, return to the boil and cook for 10 minutes. Remove with a slotted spoon and drain on kitchen paper, then transfer to a warmed serving dish. Sprinkle the tortellini with the extra grated Parmesan cheese and serve immediately.

fruity chicken fusilli

⏲ **cook: 35 mins**   ⏱ **prep: 15 mins, plus 30 mins marinating**   **serves 4**

In this delicious, summery dish, the flavour of the chicken is enhanced by the addition of juicy cubes of mango and a range of exotic spices.

NUTRITIONAL INFORMATION	
Calories	.470
Protein	.34g
Carbohydrate	.65g
Sugars	.14g
Fat	.11g
Saturates	.2g

variation

Substitute the mango with a ripe papaya, peeled, deseeded and diced, and replace the raisins with the same amount of sultanas.

INGREDIENTS

450 g/1 lb skinless, boneless chicken, diced

1 tsp ground turmeric

¼ tsp ground cinnamon

¼ tsp ground cumin

¼ tsp ground cardamom

pinch of cayenne pepper

2 tbsp groundnut oil

1 onion, finely chopped

2 garlic cloves, finely chopped

350 ml/12 fl oz Chicken Stock (see page 12)

salt

25 g/1 oz raisins

1 ripe mango, peeled, stoned and diced

280 g/10 oz dried fusilli

2 tbsp chopped fresh coriander, to garnish

1 Place the chicken in a shallow dish. Sprinkle with the turmeric, cinnamon, cumin, cardamom and cayenne and toss well to coat. Cover with clingfilm and leave to stand in the refrigerator for 30 minutes.

2 Heat the groundnut oil in a heavy-based frying pan. Add the onion and garlic and cook over a low heat, stirring occasionally, for 5 minutes, or until softened. Add the spiced chicken and cook, stirring frequently, for 5 minutes, or until golden brown all over. Pour in the Chicken Stock and season to taste with salt. Bring to the boil, add the raisins and mango, partially cover and simmer for 25 minutes.

3 Meanwhile, bring a large heavy-based saucepan of lightly salted water to the boil. Add the pasta, return to the boil and cook for 8–10 minutes, or until tender but still firm to the bite. Drain and transfer to a warmed serving dish. Add the chicken mixture, toss lightly and serve, garnished with chopped coriander.

cook's tip

You can use meat from the breast, thighs or drumsticks for this dish, if you like. Cooking the chicken first ensures that all the flavours are sealed in.

pappardelle with chicken & porcini

serves 4 | **prep: 15 mins, plus 20 mins soaking** | **cook: 50 mins**

Porcini mushrooms, also known as ceps, have a wonderful rich, deep flavour. They dry very successfully, remaining redolent of the countryside when reconstituted in hot water.

INGREDIENTS

40 g/1½ oz dried porcini mushrooms

175 ml/6 fl oz hot water

800 g/1 lb 12 oz canned chopped tomatoes

1 fresh red chilli, deseeded and finely chopped

3 tbsp olive oil

350 g/12 oz skinless, boneless chicken, cut into thin strips

2 garlic cloves, finely chopped

350 g/12 oz dried pappardelle

salt and pepper

2 tbsp chopped fresh flat-leaved parsley, to garnish

NUTRITIONAL INFORMATION

Calories 540

Protein 33g

Carbohydrate 78g

Sugars 9g

Fat 13g

Saturates 2g

cook's tip

Wild mushrooms are used extensively in Italian dishes and porcini mushrooms are the most popular. When using porcini, always soak them first in warm water for 30 minutes, then drain well before cooking.

1 Place the porcini in a small bowl, add the hot water and leave to soak for 20 minutes. Meanwhile, place the tomatoes and their can juices in a heavy-based saucepan and break them up with a wooden spoon, then stir in the chilli. Bring to the boil, reduce the heat and simmer, stirring occasionally, for 30 minutes, or until reduced.

2 Remove the mushrooms from their soaking liquid with a slotted spoon, reserving the liquid. Sieve the liquid through a coffee filter paper or muslin-lined sieve into the tomatoes and simmer for a further 15 minutes. Meanwhile, heat 2 tablespoons of the olive oil in a heavy-based frying pan. Add the chicken and cook, stirring frequently, until golden brown all over and tender. Stir in the mushrooms and garlic and cook for a further 5 minutes.

3 While the chicken is cooking, bring a large heavy-based saucepan of lightly salted water to the boil. Add the pasta, return to the boil and cook for 8–10 minutes, or until tender but still firm to the bite. Drain well, transfer to a warmed serving dish, drizzle with the remaining olive oil and toss lightly. Stir the chicken mixture into the tomato sauce, season to taste with salt and pepper and spoon on to the pasta. Toss lightly, sprinkle with parsley and serve immediately.

curried chicken fusilli

⏲ **cook: 25 mins**　　　　⏱ **prep: 15 mins**　　　　**serves 4**

This is a good way to use up leftover roast chicken and is an easy, but tasty dish for a midweek supper. Other types of pasta would also work well in this dish, such as farfalle, penne or conchiglie.

NUTRITIONAL INFORMATION	
Calories	.600
Protein	.47g
Carbohydrate	.54g
Sugars	.3g
Fat	.23g
Saturates	.8g

INGREDIENTS

25 g/1 oz butter

25 g/1 oz plain flour

450 ml/16 fl oz Chicken Stock (see page 12)

1 tbsp curry paste

175 g/6 oz mushrooms, sliced

450 g/1 lb cooked chicken, minced

salt and pepper

55 g/2 oz flaked almonds

250 g/9 oz dried fusilli bucati

4 tbsp half-fat crème fraîche

cook's tip

You can dice the chicken finely if you do not have a mincer or food processor. When frying the almonds, keep a close watch on them as they can easily burn.

1 Melt the butter in a heavy-based saucepan. Sprinkle in the flour and cook, stirring constantly, for 1 minute. Remove the saucepan from the heat and gradually whisk in the Chicken Stock. Return the saucepan to the heat, stir in the curry paste and bring to the boil, whisking constantly. Add the mushrooms and chicken, season to taste

with salt and pepper, reduce the heat and simmer gently for 15 minutes.

2 Meanwhile, dry-fry the almonds in a heavy-based frying pan over a low heat, stirring frequently, until golden. Bring a large heavy-based saucepan of lightly salted water to the boil. Add the pasta, return to the boil and

cook for 8–10 minutes, or until tender but still firm to the bite. Drain well, then transfer to a warmed serving dish.

3 Stir the crème fraîche into the chicken mixture and heat through for 1 minute. Spoon the curried chicken on to the pasta, toss lightly and serve, garnished with the toasted almonds.

fettuccine with two sauces

serves 4   **prep: 20 mins**   **cook: 30 mins**

This pretty dish is the perfect choice for a dinner party – and it tastes as delicious as it looks. For an even more striking effect, use tomato, spinach, wild mushroom or beetroot pasta rather than plain.

INGREDIENTS

250 g/9 oz dried fettuccine

salt

fresh basil sprigs, to garnish

RED SAUCE

2 tbsp olive oil

2 shallots, chopped

1 garlic clove, chopped

400 g/14 oz canned chopped tomatoes

2 tbsp shredded fresh basil

2 bay leaves

2 tbsp tomato purée

1 tsp sugar

salt and pepper

WHITE SAUCE

60 g/2¼ oz butter

400 g/14 oz skinless, boneless chicken breasts, cut into thin strips

90 g/3¼ oz flaked almonds

300 ml/10 fl oz double cream or panna da cucina

salt and pepper

variation

Replace the tomato purée with the same amount of sun-dried tomato paste and use fresh tomatoes, peeled and chopped, instead of canned ones.

cook's tip

If possible, always use fresh herbs, as they have a much better flavour than dried. If fresh are unavailable, use freeze-dried herbs instead, which can be found in most large supermarkets.

1 To make the red sauce, heat the olive oil in a heavy-based saucepan. Add the shallots and cook over a low heat, stirring occasionally, for 5 minutes. Add the garlic and cook for a further 1 minute. Stir in the tomatoes, basil, bay leaves, tomato purée and sugar and season to taste with salt and pepper. Bring the mixture to the boil, then reduce the heat and simmer for 20 minutes, or until reduced by half.

2 Meanwhile, make the chicken sauce. Melt the butter in a frying pan, add the chicken and almonds and cook over a medium heat, stirring constantly, for 5–6 minutes, or until the chicken is browned all over and tender. Pour the cream into a small saucepan and bring to the boil. Reduce the heat to low and cook for 10 minutes, or until reduced by half. Stir the cream into the chicken mixture and season to taste with salt and pepper.

3 While the white sauce is cooking, bring a large heavy-based saucepan of lightly salted water to the boil. Add the pasta, return to the boil and cook for 8–10 minutes, or until tender but still firm to the bite. Drain well and transfer to a warmed serving platter. Remove the bay leaves from the red sauce and spoon it along each side of the platter. Spoon the white sauce along the centre. Garnish with basil sprigs and serve.

orecchiette with chicken, chillies & mushrooms

cook: 25 mins **prep: 15 mins** **serves 6**

Fiery dried chillies feature in a number of southern Italian pasta sauces, naturally partnered by tomatoes that flourish in the region.

NUTRITIONAL INFORMATION

Calories	.390
Protein	.16g
Carbohydrate	.62g
Sugars	.8g
Fat	.9g
Saturates	.1g

variation

Instead of canned tomatoes, quarter 1.25 kg/2 lb 12 oz plum tomatoes. Add to the chillies with 4 tablespoons water. Proceed as in main recipe.

INGREDIENTS

800 g/1 lb 12 oz canned chopped tomatoes

4 dried red chillies

3 tbsp olive oil

1 onion, chopped

115 g/4 oz skinless, boneless chicken breast, cut into thin strips

350 g/12 oz mushrooms, sliced

3 garlic cloves, finely chopped

55 g/2 oz black olives

125 ml/4 fl oz dry white wine

450 g/1 lb dried orecchiette

2 tbsp chopped fresh flat-leaved parsley

salt and pepper

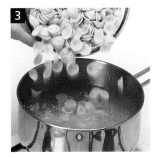

cook's tip

When rubbing the tomatoes through a sieve into a bowl, use the back of a wooden spoon to push them through. It is best to use a non-metallic sieve, as the metal may taint the flavour.

1 Place the tomatoes and their can juices in a large heavy-based saucepan with the chillies. Bring to the boil, then simmer gently for 20 minutes, or until reduced.

2 Meanwhile, heat 2 tablespoons of the olive oil in a heavy-based frying pan. Add the onion and cook over a low heat, stirring occasionally, for 5 minutes, or until softened. Add the chicken and cook, stirring frequently, for 8 minutes, or until golden brown. Add the mushrooms and garlic and cook, stirring frequently, for a further 5 minutes. Add the olives and wine and cook for 3–5 minutes, or until reduced.

3 While the chicken mixture is cooking, bring a large heavy-based saucepan of lightly salted water to the boil. Add the pasta, return to the boil and cook for 8–10 minutes, or until tender but still firm to the bite. Rub the tomato and chilli mixture through a sieve into a bowl and reserve.

4 Drain the pasta well and transfer to a warmed serving dish. Stir the reserved tomato sauce into the chicken mixture with the parsley, season to taste with salt and pepper and spoon over the pasta. Toss lightly and serve.

garganelli with chicken & feta

serves 4   **prep: 10 mins**   **cook: 10 mins**

This unusual combination makes a simple and enjoyable midweek supper that is just right for warm summer evenings.

INGREDIENTS

2 tbsp olive oil

450 g/1 lb skinless, boneless chicken breasts, cut into thin strips

6 spring onions, chopped

225 g/8 oz feta cheese, diced

4 tbsp snipped fresh chives

salt and pepper

450 g/1 lb dried garganelli

NUTRITIONAL INFORMATION

Calories 700

Protein 48g

Carbohydrate 84g

Sugars 4g

Fat 22g

Saturates 2g

variation

Substitute diced, firm, white fish fillet such as monkfish for the chicken and replace the garganelli with either penne or pipe rigate, if you like.

1 Heat the olive oil in a heavy-based frying pan. Add the chicken and cook over a medium heat, stirring frequently, for 5–8 minutes, or until golden all over and cooked through. Add the spring onions and cook for 2 minutes. Stir the feta cheese into the frying pan with half the chives and season to taste with salt and pepper.

2 Meanwhile, bring a large heavy-based saucepan of lightly salted water to the boil. Add the pasta, return to the boil and cook for 8–10 minutes, or until tender but still firm to the bite. Drain well, then transfer to a warmed serving dish.

3 Spoon the chicken mixture on to the pasta, toss lightly and serve immediately, garnished with the remaining chives.

tuscan chicken tagliarini

⏱ **cook: 45 mins**   ⏱ **prep: 15 mins**   **serves 4**

Simplicity is the keynote of Tuscan cuisine – and this means using the best and freshest ingredients for a memorable meal.

NUTRITIONAL INFORMATION	
Calories	.570
Protein	.40g
Carbohydrate	.76g
Sugars	.10g
Fat	.11g
Saturates	.2g

INGREDIENTS

2 tbsp olive oil

4 skinless, boneless chicken breasts

1 onion, thinly sliced

2 red peppers, deseeded and sliced

1 garlic clove, finely chopped

300 ml/10 fl oz passata

150 ml/5 fl oz dry white wine

1 tbsp chopped fresh marjoram

salt and pepper

350 g/12 oz dried tagliarini

400 g/14 oz canned cannellini beans, drained and rinsed

variation

Use 450 g/1 lb peeled raw prawns instead of chicken. Cook them in oil in Step 1 until they turn pink, then reserve. Return to the pan with the beans in Step 3.

1 Heat half the olive oil in a heavy-based frying pan. Add the chicken and cook over a medium heat for 4 minutes, or until golden brown on all sides. Remove from the frying pan and keep warm. Reduce the heat, add the onion and red peppers to the frying pan and cook, stirring occasionally, for 5 minutes, or until softened.

Stir in the garlic. Return the chicken to the frying pan, add the passata, wine and marjoram and season to taste with salt and pepper. Cover and simmer gently, stirring occasionally, for 30 minutes, or until the chicken is tender.

2 Meanwhile, bring a large heavy-based saucepan of lightly salted

water to the boil. Add the pasta, return to the boil and cook for 8–10 minutes, or until tender but still firm to the bite. Drain well, return to the saucepan, drizzle with the remaining oil and toss lightly.

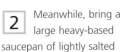 **3** Stir the cannellini beans into the chicken mixture and simmer for 5 minutes, or until heated through. Divide

the pasta between individual serving plates and top with the chicken sauce. Serve.

penne with chicken & rocket

serves 4   **prep: 15 mins**   **cook: 25 mins**

*The sharp, peppery flavour of rocket contrasts with the creamy
richness of the sauce in this aromatic dish.*

INGREDIENTS

25 g/1 oz butter	salt and pepper
2 carrots, cut into thin batons	2 tbsp cornflour
1 small onion, finely chopped	4 tbsp water
225 g/8 oz skinless, boneless	2 tbsp single cream
chicken breast, diced	125 ml/4 fl oz natural yogurt
225 g/8 oz mushrooms, quartered	2 tsp fresh thyme leaves
125 ml/4 fl oz dry white wine	115 g/4 oz rocket
125 ml/4 fl oz Chicken Stock	350 g/12 oz dried penne
(see page 12)	fresh thyme sprigs, to garnish
2 garlic cloves, finely chopped	

NUTRITIONAL INFORMATION

Calories 555

Protein 27g

Carbohydrate 87g

Sugars 10g

Fat 11g

Saturates 5g

---

variation

Replace the rocket with the same
amount of fresh watercress or baby
spinach leaves, if you prefer.

cook's tip

For a meatier dish, use chicken
or turkey thighs and cook for
slightly longer, until the meat is
thoroughly cooked through.
If you prefer a strong garlic
flavour, then finely slice the
garlic instead of chopping it.

1 Melt the butter in a
heavy-based frying pan.
Add the carrots and cook over
a medium heat, stirring
frequently, for 2 minutes.
Add the onion, chicken,
mushrooms, wine, Chicken
Stock and garlic and season to
taste with salt and pepper. Mix
the cornflour and water
together in a bowl until a
smooth paste forms, then stir

in the cream and yogurt. Stir
the cornflour mixture into the
frying pan with the thyme,
cover and simmer for 5
minutes. Place the rocket on
top of the chicken, but do not
stir in, cover and cook for 5
minutes, or until the chicken is
tender.

2 Sieve the cooking liquid
into a clean saucepan,

then transfer the chicken and
vegetables to a dish and keep
warm. Heat the cooking
liquid, whisking occasionally,
for 10 minutes, or until
reduced and thickened.

3 Meanwhile, bring a
large heavy-based
saucepan of lightly salted
water to the boil. Add the
pasta, return to the boil and

cook for 8–10 minutes, or until
tender but still firm to the bite.
Return the chicken and
vegetables to the thickened
cooking liquid and stir to coat.

4 Drain the pasta well,
transfer to a warmed
serving dish and spoon the
chicken and vegetable mixture
on top. Garnish with thyme
sprigs and serve immediately.

fish & shellfish

We are advised by nutritionists to eat more fish – at least two meals a week – and what better way is there to enjoy it than in combination with pasta? Even fussy children, who would not contemplate tackling a fish fillet on its own, will tuck into Haddock & Pasta Bake (see page 107) or Lasagne alla Marinara (see page 102), and they may even surprise you with a new-found enthusiasm for squid or clams. Shellfish have an affinity with pasta, and mussels, clams, scallops and prawns feature in many classic recipes, such as Fettuccine with Saffron Mussels (see page 119) and Spaghetti con Vongole (see page 122).

The versatility of pasta is matched by the versatility of fish and shellfish, providing endless scope for marvellous meals. Recipes range from quick and easy store cupboard dishes, such as Spaghettini with Quick Tuna Sauce (see page 98), to the time-consuming but truly wonderful Crab Ravioli (see page 114), and from the cheap and cheerful Linguine with Sardines (see page 96) to the utterly outrageous Spaghetti with Prawns & Caviar (see page 127). As well as fabulous fish sauces served with long or short pasta and substantial layered bakes, you will find unusual pasta parcels and even a Pasta Omelette with Prawns (see page 124). Whatever the occasion or time of year, pasta with seafood will provide a nourishing, satisfying and, above all, delicious meal.

linguine with sardines

Quick and easy, yet packed full of flavour, this pasta dish can be made entirely from store cupboard ingredients for a midweek supper when you have been too busy to think about planning the meal.

INGREDIENTS

4 tbsp olive oil

1 small onion, finely chopped

55 g/2 oz canned anchovy fillets, drained

400 g/14 oz canned chopped tomatoes

25 g/1 oz pine kernels

250 g/9 oz canned sardines in oil, drained

salt and pepper

350 g/12 oz dried linguine

55 g/2 oz dried, uncoloured breadcrumbs

NUTRITIONAL INFORMATION

Calories	.655
Protein	.29g
Carbohydrate	.80g
Sugars	.8g
Fat	.27g
Saturates	.3g

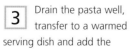

cook's tip

If you have any fresh herbs, such as flat-leaved parsley or thyme, chop 1–2 tablespoons and add with the breadcrumbs in Step 3.

1   Heat the olive oil in a large, heavy-based frying pan. Add the onion and anchovies and cook over a low heat, stirring occasionally, for 5 minutes, or until the onion is softened. Add the pine kernels and tomatoes and simmer gently for 10 minutes. Add the sardines, season to taste with salt and pepper and simmer for a further 5 minutes.

2   Meanwhile, bring a large, heavy-based saucepan of lightly salted water to the boil. Add the pasta, return to the boil and cook for 8–10 minutes, or until tender but still firm to the bite.

3   Drain the pasta well, transfer to a warmed serving dish and add the sardine mixture and the breadcrumbs. Toss lightly and serve immediately.

mafalde with fresh salmon

cook: 25 mins   **prep: 15 mins**   **serves 4**

While this creamy combination of fresh salmon and prawns may seem quite extravagant, a little goes a long way. This dish is perfect for an informal dinner party, if served with a crisp green salad.

NUTRITIONAL INFORMATION

Calories 716

Protein 35g

Carbohydrate 70g

Sugars 8g

Fat 31g

Saturates 13g

INGREDIENTS

350 g/12 oz salmon fillet

fresh dill sprigs, plus extra to garnish

225 ml/8 fl oz dry white wine

salt and pepper

6 tomatoes, peeled and chopped

150 ml/5 fl oz double cream or panna da cucina

350 g/12 oz dried mafalde

115 g/4 oz cooked, peeled prawns

cook's tip

If using frozen prawns, make sure that they are completely thawed before using. If you are unable to find mafalde pasta, then use pappardelle instead.

1 Place the salmon in a large heavy-based frying pan. Add a few dill sprigs, pour in the wine and season to taste with salt and pepper. Bring to the boil, then reduce the heat, cover and poach gently for 5 minutes, or until the flesh flakes easily. Remove with a fish slice, reserving the cooking liquid, and leave to cool slightly. Remove and discard the skin and any remaining small bones, then flake the flesh into large chunks.

2 Add the tomatoes and cream to the reserved liquid. Bring to the boil, then reduce the heat and simmer for 15 minutes, or until thickened.

3 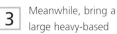 Meanwhile, bring a large heavy-based saucepan of lightly salted water to the boil. Add the pasta, return to the boil and cook for 8–10 minutes, or until tender but still firm to the bite. Drain and transfer to a warmed serving dish.

4 Add the salmon and prawns to the tomato mixture and stir gently until coated in the sauce. Spoon the salmon sauce on to the pasta, toss lightly, then serve, garnished with dill sprigs.

spaghettini with quick tuna sauce

serves 4   **prep: 20 mins** ⟲   **cook: 30 mins** ⟲

Canned fish is such a useful and versatile ingredient. Here, canned tuna is combined with fresh tomatoes, mushrooms and herbs to make a scrumptious pasta sauce.

INGREDIENTS

3 tbsp olive oil

4 tomatoes, peeled, deseeded and roughly chopped

115 g/4 oz mushrooms, sliced

1 tbsp shredded fresh basil

400 g/14 oz canned tuna, drained

100 ml/3½ fl oz Fish Stock or Chicken Stock (see page 12)

1 garlic clove, finely chopped

2 tsp chopped fresh marjoram

salt and pepper

350 g/12 oz dried spaghettini

115 g/4 oz freshly grated Parmesan cheese, to serve

NUTRITIONAL INFORMATION

Calories 600

Protein 35g

Carbohydrate 68g

Sugars 6g

Fat 24g

Saturates 8g

variation

Use other canned fish such as salmon instead of the tuna, and replace the shredded fresh basil with the same amount of finely chopped fresh parsley.

cook's tip

If fresh ingredients are limited, use 400 g/14 oz canned chopped tomatoes and a low-salt stock cube. You could also substitute 1 teaspoon chopped preserved garlic or a pinch of garlic powder for the fresh clove.

1 Heat the olive oil in a large frying pan. Add the tomatoes and cook over a low heat, stirring occasionally, for 15 minutes, or until pulpy. Add the mushrooms and cook, stirring occasionally, for a further 10 minutes. Stir in the basil, tuna, Fish Stock, garlic and marjoram and season to taste with salt and pepper. Cook over a low heat for 5 minutes, or until heated through.

2 Meanwhile, bring a large heavy-based saucepan of lightly salted water to the boil. Add the pasta, return to the boil and cook for 8–10 minutes, or until tender but still firm to the bite.

3 Drain the pasta well, transfer to a warmed serving dish and spoon on the tuna mixture. Serve with grated Parmesan cheese.

fettuccine alla bucaniera

⏱ **cook: 50 mins**　　　🕐 **prep: 20 mins**　　　**serves 6**

variation

You can substitute plaice or dab for the sole fillets and haddock or cod for the monkfish, if you like.

This classic, yet simple recipe brings out both the delicate flavour of sole and the more robust taste of monkfish.

INGREDIENTS

85 g/3 oz plain flour	1 carrot, diced
salt and pepper	1 leek, finely chopped
450 g/1 lb lemon sole fillets, skinned and cut into chunks	300 ml/10 fl oz Fish Stock (see page 12)
450 g/1 lb monkfish fillets, skinned and cut into chunks	300 ml/10 fl oz dry white wine
	2 tsp anchovy essence
85 g/3 oz unsalted butter	1 tbsp balsamic vinegar
4 shallots, finely chopped	450 g/1 lb dried fettuccine
2 garlic cloves, crushed	chopped fresh flat-leaved parsley, to garnish

cook's tip

Make sure you remove the grey membrane, as well as the skin, from the monkfish before cooking. The white membrane helps to hold the fish pieces together during cooking.

1 Season the flour with salt and pepper and spread out 25 g/1 oz on a plate. Coat all the fish pieces with it, shaking off the excess. Melt the butter in a heavy-based saucepan or flameproof casserole. Add the fish, shallots, garlic, carrot and leek, then cook over a low heat, stirring frequently, for 10 minutes. Sprinkle in the remaining seasoned flour and cook, stirring constantly, for 1 minute.

2 Mix the Fish Stock, wine, anchovy essence and balsamic vinegar together in a jug and gradually stir into the fish mixture. Bring to the boil, stirring constantly, then reduce the heat and simmer gently for 35 minutes.

3 Meanwhile, bring a large heavy-based saucepan of lightly salted water to the boil. Add the pasta, return to the boil and cook for 8–10 minutes, or until tender but still firm to the bite. Drain and transfer to a warmed serving dish. Spoon the fish mixture on to the pasta, garnish with chopped parsley and serve immediately.

lasagne alla marinara

serves 6   prep: 20 mins   cook: 45 mins

This lasagne looks, tastes and smells wonderful and makes an excellent choice for informal entertaining.

INGREDIENTS

15 g/½ oz butter	salt and pepper
225 g/8 oz raw prawns, peeled, deveined and roughly chopped	400 g/14 oz canned chopped tomatoes
450 g/1 lb monkfish fillets, skinned and chopped	1 tbsp chopped fresh chervil
	1 tbsp shredded fresh basil
225 g/8 oz chestnut mushrooms, chopped	175 g/6 oz dried no-pre-cook lasagne
850 ml/1½ pints Béchamel Sauce (see page 12)	85 g/3 oz freshly grated Parmesan cheese

variation

If fresh chervil is unavailable, then use tarragon, dill or parsley instead. Spinach-flavoured lasagne would also work well in this dish.

cook's tip

This filling would be ideal to use in dried cannelloni tubes with a sauce of your choice. Cut the fish and prawns into small pieces, otherwise it may be difficult to fill the tubes.

1 Preheat the oven to 190°C/375°F/Gas Mark 5. Melt the butter in a large heavy-based saucepan. Add the prawns and monkfish and cook over a medium heat for 3–5 minutes, or until the prawns change colour. Transfer the prawns to a small heatproof bowl with a slotted spoon. Add the mushrooms to the saucepan and cook, stirring occasionally, for 5 minutes. Transfer the fish and mushrooms to the bowl.

2 Stir the fish mixture, with any juices, into the Béchamel Sauce and season to taste with salt and pepper. Layer the tomatoes, chervil, basil, fish mixture and lasagne sheets in a large ovenproof dish, ending with a layer of the fish mixture. Sprinkle evenly with the grated Parmesan cheese.

3 Bake in the preheated oven for 35 minutes, or until golden brown, then serve immediately.

italian fish stew with ziti

serves 4   **prep: 20 mins**   **cook: 20 mins**

Whether you are entertaining or just cooking for the family, this light and refreshing dish is the perfect meal at any time of the year.

INGREDIENTS

pinch of saffron threads

1 litre/1¾ pints Fish Stock

(see page 12)

55 g/2 oz butter

450 g/1 lb red mullet fillets,

thinly sliced

12 prepared scallops

12 raw tiger prawns, peeled

and deveined

225 g/8 oz raw prawns, peeled

and deveined

salt and pepper

finely grated rind and juice of 1 lemon

150 ml/5 fl oz white wine vinegar

150 ml/5 fl oz white wine

150 ml/5 fl oz double cream or

panna da cucina

3 tbsp chopped fresh

flat-leaved parsley

450 g/1 lb dried ziti

variation

Replace the red mullet with red snapper. Other types of pasta would also work well in this dish, such as tortiglioni or campanelle.

cook's tip

Use a mixture of different-sized prawns for an authentic Italian dish. There are many varieties available in Italy, from the tiny *gamberetti* to *gamberoni* – the Mediterranean equivalent of tiger prawns.

1 Place the saffron in a small bowl, add 3 table-spoons of the Fish Stock and leave to soak. Melt the butter in a large heavy-based saucepan or flameproof casserole. Add the red mullet, scallops and both types of prawns and cook over a medium heat, stirring frequently, for 3–5 minutes, or until the prawns have changed colour. Season to taste with pepper and add the grated rind and lemon juice. Transfer the fish and shellfish to a plate and keep warm.

2 Pour the remaining stock into the saucepan and add the saffron and its soaking liquid. Bring to the boil and cook until reduced by about one-third. Add the vinegar and continue to boil for 4 minutes. Stir in the white wine and cook for 5 minutes, or until reduced and thickened. Add the cream and parsley, then season to taste with salt and pepper and simmer gently for 2 minutes.

3 Meanwhile, bring a large heavy-based saucepan of lightly salted water to the boil. Add the pasta, return to the boil and cook for 8–10 minutes, or until tender but still firm to the bite. Drain well and transfer to a warmed serving platter. Arrange the fish and shellfish on top and pour over the sauce. Serve immediately.

bavettini with smoked salmon & rocket

serves 4   **prep: 10 mins**   **cook: 10 mins**

*Pasta with attitude – this simple and elegant dish is pure perfection.
Serve with a fresh green salad for a filling lunch.*

INGREDIENTS

350 g/12 oz dried bavettini

2 tbsp olive oil

1 garlic clove, finely chopped

115 g/4 oz smoked salmon,
cut into thin strips

55 g/2 oz rocket

salt and pepper

NUTRITIONAL INFORMATION

Calories 395

Protein 18g

Carbohydrate 65g

Sugars 3g

Fat 9g

Saturates 1g

cook's tip

Do not overcook the salmon or rocket; they should just be warmed through and the rocket lightly wilted. If rocket is unavailable, use baby spinach leaves instead.

1 Bring a large heavy-based saucepan of lightly salted water to the boil. Add the pasta, return to the boil and cook for 8–10 minutes, or until tender but still firm to the bite.

2 Just before the end of the cooking time, heat the olive oil in a heavy-based frying pan. Add the garlic and cook over a low heat, stirring constantly, for 1 minute. Do not allow the garlic to brown or it will taste bitter. Add the salmon and rocket. Season to taste with pepper and cook, stirring constantly, for 1 minute. Remove the frying pan from the heat.

3 Drain the pasta and transfer to a warmed serving dish. Add the smoked salmon and rocket mixture, toss lightly and serve.

haddock & pasta bake

⏱ **cook: 25 mins** 　　　 ⏱ **prep: 20 mins** 　　　 **serves 4**

Warming, filling and comforting, this is just the right dish for a family supper in the middle of winter.

NUTRITIONAL INFORMATION

Calories 787

Protein 44g

Carbohydrate 98g

Sugars 10g

Fat 27g

Saturates 15g

INGREDIENTS

25g/1 oz butter, plus extra for greasing

450 g/1 lb smoked haddock fillets, thickly sliced

600 ml/1 pint milk

1 bay leaf

4 juniper berries

2 hard-boiled eggs, shelled

25 g/1 oz plain flour

pinch of cayenne pepper

salt and pepper

2 tsp lemon juice

3 tbsp double cream

1 tbsp chopped fresh parsley

450 g/1 lb dried elbow macaroni

cook's tip

Look for undyed smoked haddock, which is a more attractive colour, has a better flavour and is healthier. It is usually available in most large supermarkets.

1 Preheat the oven to 200°C/400°F/Gas Mark 6. Grease a large ovenproof dish with butter. Place the fish in the dish, pour in the milk and add the bay leaf and juniper berries. Cover and bake in the preheated oven for 15 minutes.

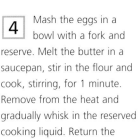

2 Just before the fish is cooked, bring a large heavy-based saucepan of lightly salted water to the boil. Add the pasta, then return to the boil and cook for 8–10 minutes, or until tender but still firm to the bite.

3 Meanwhile, remove the fish from the oven, but do not switch the oven off. Carefully pour the cooking liquid into a jug without breaking up the fish. Remove and discard the bay leaf and juniper berries.

4 Mash the eggs in a bowl with a fork and reserve. Melt the butter in a saucepan, stir in the flour and cook, stirring, for 1 minute. Remove from the heat and gradually whisk in the reserved cooking liquid. Return the saucepan to the heat and season to taste with cayenne, salt and pepper. Stir in the lemon juice, cream, parsley and mashed egg and cook, stirring constantly, for 2 minutes.

5 Drain the pasta and spoon it over the fish. Pour the sauce over the top and bake in the preheated oven for 10 minutes. Serve.

tagliatelle with hake in chilli sauce

serves 4 **prep: 10 mins** **cook: 20 mins**

The surprisingly delicate flavour of this light, summery dish would make it a good choice for an al fresco lunch.

INGREDIENTS

bunch of fresh parsley

1 garlic clove, finely chopped

1 dried red chilli, deseeded

5 tbsp olive oil

450 g/1 lb hake fillets, skinned and cut into chunks

350 g/12 oz tomatoes, peeled, deseeded and diced

salt and pepper

350 g/12 oz dried tagliatelle

NUTRITIONAL INFORMATION

Calories	.544
Protein	.32g
Carbohydrate	.68g
Sugars	.6g
Fat	.18g
Saturates	.2g

cook's tip

Make sure that you remove any fine bones remaining in the fish fillets. This is most easily done with tweezers.

1 Using a sharp knife, chop the parsley, garlic and chilli together. Heat half the olive oil in a large heavy-based frying pan, add the herb mixture and cook over a low heat, stirring, for 1–2 minutes, or until the garlic gives off its aroma. Add the fish, cover and cook for 5 minutes, then turn the fish and cook for a further 5 minutes. Add the tomatoes and season to taste with salt and pepper. Re-cover the frying pan and simmer for a further 5 minutes.

2 Meanwhile, bring a large heavy-based saucepan of lightly salted water to the boil. Add the pasta, return to the boil and cook for 8–10 minutes, or until tender but still firm to the bite.

3 Drain the pasta, return to the saucepan, drizzle with the remaining olive oil and toss. Transfer to a warmed serving platter and top with the fish mixture. Serve immediately.

fusilli with monkfish & broccoli

⏲ **cook: 15 mins**   ◔ **prep: 10 mins**   **serves 4**

This filling, clean-tasting dish is easy to make and takes so little time that it is ideal for a midweek family supper.

NUTRITIONAL INFORMATION	
Calories	.830
Protein	.32g
Carbohydrate	.77g
Sugars	.6g
Fat	.44g
Saturates	.22g

INGREDIENTS

115 g/4 oz broccoli, divided into florets

3 tbsp olive oil

350 g/12 oz monkfish fillet, skinned
and cut into bite-sized pieces

2 garlic cloves, crushed

salt and pepper

125 ml/4 fl oz dry white wine

225 ml/8 fl oz double cream or
panna da cucina

400 g/14 oz dried fusilli bucati

85 g/3 oz Gorgonzola cheese, diced

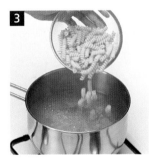

variation

Substitute skinless, boneless chicken breasts for the monkfish and fusilli instead of fusilli bucati, if you prefer.

1 Divide the broccoli florets into tiny sprigs. Bring a saucepan of lightly salted water to the boil, add the broccoli and cook for 2 minutes. Drain and refresh under cold running water.

2 Heat the olive oil in a large heavy-based frying pan. Add the monkfish and garlic and season to taste with salt and pepper. Cook, stirring frequently, for 5 minutes, or until the fish is opaque. Pour in the white wine and cream and cook, stirring occasionally, for 5 minutes, or until the fish is cooked through and the sauce has thickened. Stir in the broccoli sprigs.

3 Meanwhile, bring a large heavy-based saucepan of lightly salted water to the boil. Add the pasta, return to the boil and cook for 8–10 minutes, or until tender but still firm to the bite. Drain and tip the pasta into the saucepan with the fish, add the cheese and toss lightly. Serve immediately.

creamy smoked trout tagliatelle

serves 6   **prep: 15 mins**   **cook: 15 mins**

Contrasting colours and textures make this a good choice for family meals and for informal entertaining.

INGREDIENTS

2 carrots, cut into thin batons

2 celery sticks, cut into thin batons

1 courgette, cut into thin batons

1 leek, cut into thin batons

115 g/4 oz peas

150 ml/5 fl oz Vegetable Stock

(see page 12)

225 g/8 oz smoked trout fillets, skinned and cut into thin strips

200 g/7 oz cream cheese

150 ml/5 fl oz dry white wine

2 tbsp snipped fresh dill

salt and pepper

225 g/8 oz dried tagliatelle

fresh dill sprigs, to garnish

NUTRITIONAL INFORMATION

Calories	.370
Protein	.16g
Carbohydrate	.33g
Sugars	.4g
Fat	.19g
Saturates	.10g

variation

You could use other smoked fish, such as buckling, halibut or swordfish, instead of the smoked trout.

cook's tip

Dried pasta swells to nearly double its size when cooked, so it is best to use a large colander, preferably with a long handle, to drain it.

1 Place the carrots, celery, courgette, leek and peas into a large heavy-based saucepan and pour in the Vegetable Stock. Bring to the boil, reduce the heat and simmer for 5 minutes, or until tender and most of the stock has evaporated. Remove the saucepan from the heat, stir in the smoked trout and cover to keep warm.

2 Place the cheese and wine in a separate large heavy-based saucepan and stir over a low heat until the cheese has melted and the mixture is smooth. Stir in the snipped dill and season to taste with salt and pepper.

3 Meanwhile, bring a large heavy-based saucepan of lightly salted water to the boil. Add the pasta, return to the boil and cook for 8–10 minutes, or until tender but still firm to the bite. Drain and tip the pasta into the cheese sauce. Toss well to coat, then transfer to a warmed serving dish. Top with the smoked trout mixture, garnish with dill sprigs and serve immediately.

shellfish bake

cook: 35 mins   **prep: 20 mins**   **serves 6**

variation

Substitute the conchiglie with other types of small pasta shapes, such as orechiette, if you prefer.

This lovely, light bake is a summertime treat and needs only a crisp salad and some crusty bread to make a filling meal.

INGREDIENTS

salt

350 g/12 oz dried conchiglie

85 g/3 oz butter, plus extra

for greasing

2 fennel bulbs, thinly sliced

and fronds reserved

175 g/6 oz mushrooms, thinly sliced

175 g/6 oz cooked peeled prawns

175 g/6 oz crabmeat

pinch of cayenne pepper

300 ml/10 fl oz Béchamel Sauce

(see page 12)

55 g/2 oz freshly grated

Parmesan cheese

2 beef tomatoes, sliced

olive oil, for brushing

green salad, to serve

cook's tip

You can either use cooked fresh crabmeat or canned. If you wish to use fresh crab and time is limited, buy a ready-dressed crab from your fishmonger.

1 Preheat the oven to 180°C/350°F/Gas Mark 4. Bring a large heavy-based saucepan of lightly salted water to the boil. Add the pasta, return to the boil and cook for 8–10 minutes, or until tender but still firm to the bite. Drain well, return to the saucepan and stir in 25 g/ 1 oz of the butter. Cover and keep warm.

2 Meanwhile, melt the remaining butter in a large heavy-based frying pan. Add the fennel and cook over a medium heat for 5 minutes, or until softened. Stir in the mushrooms and cook for a further 2 minutes. Stir in the prawns and crabmeat, cook for a further 1 minute, then remove the frying pan from the heat.

3 Grease 6 small ovenproof dishes with butter. Stir the cayenne pepper into the Béchamel Sauce, add the shellfish mixture and pasta, then spoon into the prepared dishes. Sprinkle with the Parmesan cheese and arrange the tomato slices on top, then brush the tomatoes with a little olive oil.

4 Bake in the preheated oven for 25 minutes, or until golden brown. Serve hot with a green salad.

crab ravioli

serves 4　　　　**prep: 30 mins, plus 1 hr resting**　　　　**cook: 30 mins**

Spicy and succulent, crab-filled ravioli are sure to impress your guests for a meal celebrating a special occasion.

INGREDIENTS

6 spring onions

350 g/12 oz crabmeat

2 tsp finely chopped fresh root ginger

⅛–¼ tsp chilli or Tabasco sauce

700 g/1 lb 9 oz tomatoes, peeled, deseeded and roughly chopped

1 garlic clove, finely chopped

1 tbsp white wine vinegar

1 quantity Basic Pasta Dough (see page 13)

plain flour, for dusting

salt

2 tbsp double cream or panna da cucina

shredded spring onion, to garnish

NUTRITIONAL INFORMATION

Calories	.450
Protein	.29g
Carbohydrate	.46g
Sugars	.7g
Fat	.19g
Saturates	.7g

variation

For a change, use tomato, beetroot or spinach-flavoured pasta instead of the plain.

1 Thinly slice the spring onions, keeping the white and green parts separate. Mix the green spring onions, crabmeat, ginger and chilli sauce to taste together in a bowl. Cover with clingfilm and leave to chill until required.

2 Place the tomatoes in a food processor and process to a purée. Place the garlic, white spring onions and vinegar in a heavy-based saucepan and add the puréed tomatoes. Bring to the boil, stirring frequently, then reduce the heat and simmer gently for 10 minutes. Remove from the heat and reserve.

3 Divide the Pasta Dough in half and roll out on a lightly floured work surface.

Make the ravioli (see page 79, Step 2), filling them with the crabmeat mixture. Place the ravioli on a tea towel and leave to rest for 1 hour.

4 Bring a large heavy-based saucepan of lightly salted water to the boil. Add the ravioli, in batches, return to the boil and cook for 5 minutes.

Remove with a slotted spoon and drain on kitchen paper. Meanwhile, gently heat the tomato sauce and whisk in the cream. Place the ravioli in a warmed serving dishes, pour the sauce over them, garnish with shredded spring onion and serve.

mussels & bucatini parcels

cook: 25 mins   **prep: 15 mins**   **serves 4**

Dishes served in paper parcels are always fun for family and friends and are a good way of ensuring that food is served really hot.

NUTRITIONAL INFORMATION

Calories 500

Protein 24g

Carbohydrate 67g

Sugars 4g

Fat 14g

Saturates 2g

INGREDIENTS

12 garlic cloves, lightly crushed,
plus 1 garlic clove, finely chopped

2 lemons, sliced

1 kg/2 lb 4 oz live mussels, scrubbed
and debearded (see Cook's Tip)

150 ml/5 fl oz dry white wine

350 g/12 oz dried bucatini

4 tbsp olive oil

4 tbsp finely chopped fresh
flat-leaved parsley

salt and pepper

4 tbsp passata

cook's tip

Before cooking, discard any mussels with broken shells or any that refuse to close when tapped. Use baking paper rather than greaseproof paper for the parcels, so that the mussels don't stick.

1 Preheat the oven to 180°C/350°C/Gas Mark 4. Cut out 4 x 25-cm/ 10-inch squares of baking paper. Place the crushed garlic, lemons and mussels in a large heavy-based saucepan and pour in the wine. Cover tightly and cook over a high heat, shaking the pan occasionally, for 5 minutes, or until the shells have opened. Remove the mussels with a slotted spoon and discard any that remain closed. Sieve the cooking liquid through a muslin-lined sieve and reserve. Remove the mussels from their shells and chop about one-third of them.

2 Bring a large heavy-based saucepan of lightly salted water to the boil. Add the pasta, return to the boil and cook for 6–8 minutes, or until nearly tender.

3 Meanwhile, heat the oil in a large frying pan. Add the chopped garlic, parsley and chopped mussels and cook, stirring, for 1 minute. Drain the pasta and add it to the frying pan with the remaining mussels and 4 tablespoons of the sieved cooking liquid. Season to taste with pepper and cook for 1 minute, then remove from the heat.

4 Divide the mixture between the paper squares. Top each portion with 1 tablespoon of passata. Fold over the edges to seal, transfer to a baking sheet and bake in the oven for 10 minutes. Serve.

mixed shellfish with angel hair pasta

A stir-fried shellfish medley with a soy sauce dressing, served on a bed of fine pasta strands, is a kind of Westernized chow mein.

INGREDIENTS

85 g/3 oz prepared squid	350 g/12 oz capelli d'angelo
1 tsp cornflour	3 tbsp groundnut oil
1 tbsp water	55 g/2 oz mangetout
1 egg white	1 tbsp dark soy sauce
4 prepared scallops, sliced	1 tbsp dry sherry
85 g/3 oz raw prawns, peeled	½ tsp light brown sugar
and deveined	2 spring onions, shredded
salt	

NUTRITIONAL INFORMATION

Calories 468

Protein 26g

Carbohydrate 70g

Sugars 4g

Fat 11g

Saturates 2g

variation

Substitute the mangetout with the same amount of sugar snap peas and use sunflower oil instead of the groundnut oil, if you prefer.

cook's tip

If you are using a wok, heat it first without any oil until hot, then add the oil and swirl it around to cover the base and sides of the wok. Preheating the wok beforehand prevents the food sticking.

1 Open out the squid and, with a sharp knife, score the inside with criss-cross lines. Cut into small pieces, about 2-cm/¾-inch square. Place in a bowl and cover with boiling water. When the squares have curled up, drain and rinse in cold water. Mix the cornflour and water together in a small bowl until a smooth paste forms and stir in about half the egg white. Add the scallops and prawns and toss until thoroughly coated.

2 Bring a large heavy-based saucepan of lightly salted water to the boil. Add the pasta, return to the boil and cook for 5 minutes, or until tender but still firm to the bite.

3 Meanwhile, heat the oil in a preheated wok or heavy-based frying pan. Add the mangetout, squid, scallops and prawns and stir-fry for 2 minutes. Stir in the soy sauce, sherry, sugar and spring onions and cook, stirring, for 1 minute. Drain the pasta and divide it between warmed plates. Top with the shellfish and serve.

shellfish & pasta parcels

serves 4   **prep: 15 mins**   **cook: 30 mins**

What more quintessentially Italian combination could there be than spaghetti, mussels, prawns and tomatoes?

INGREDIENTS

1 lemon, sliced

450 g/1 lb live mussels, scrubbed
and debearded (see Cook's Tip)

125 ml/4 fl oz dry white wine

1 tbsp olive oil

2 garlic cloves, finely chopped

450 g/1 lb tomatoes, peeled

225 g/8 oz cooked peeled prawns

2 tbsp chopped fresh parsley

salt and pepper

350 g/12 oz dried spaghetti

fresh flat-leaved parsley sprigs and
lemon halves, to garnish

NUTRITIONAL INFORMATION	
Calories 430	
Protein 30g	
Carbohydrate 69g	
Sugars 7g	
Fat 4g	
Saturates 1g	

cook's tip

Before cooking, discard any mussels with damaged or broken shells or any that refuse to close when sharply tapped with a knife.

1 Preheat the oven to 150°C/300°F/Gas Mark 2. Cut out 4 rectangles of baking paper, 30 x 46 cm/ 12 x 18 inches. Place the sliced lemon and mussels in a large heavy-based saucepan and add the wine. Cover and cook over a high heat, shaking the saucepan occasionally, for 5 minutes, or until the shells have opened. Remove the

mussels with a slotted spoon, reserving the cooking liquid. Discard any that remain closed. Sieve the liquid through a muslin-lined sieve and reserve.

2 Heat the olive oil in a frying pan, add the garlic and cook for 1 minute. Chop the tomatoes, then add to the frying pan and cook over a medium heat for

10 minutes, or until softened. Stir in the reserved cooking liquid. Reduce the heat, add the prawns and parsley and simmer for 2 minutes. Season to taste with salt and pepper.

3 Meanwhile, bring a large heavy-based saucepan of lightly salted water to the boil. Add the pasta, return to the boil and

cook for 8–10 minutes, or until tender but still firm to the bite. Drain and tip into a bowl. Add the tomato mixture and toss well. Stir in the mussels. Divide the mixture between the paper rectangles and fold over the edges to seal. Transfer to a baking sheet and cook in the oven for 10 minutes. Open up the parcels and garnish with the parsley. Serve.

fettuccine with saffron mussels

cook: 20 mins   **prep: 15 mins**   **serves 4**

A classic combination and a sophisticated pasta dish,
this looks mouthwatering and tastes superb.

NUTRITIONAL INFORMATION

Calories	.510
Protein	.29g
Carbohydrate	.76g
Sugars	.6g
Fat	.9g
Saturates	.3g

INGREDIENTS

pinch of saffron threads

175 ml/6 fl oz hot water

1 kg/2 lb 4 oz live mussels, scrubbed

and debearded (see Cook's Tip)

125 ml/4 fl oz cold water

1 tbsp sunflower oil

1 small onion, finely chopped

2 tbsp plain flour

125 ml/4 fl oz dry white vermouth

4 tbsp freshly grated Parmesan cheese

2 tbsp snipped chives, plus extra

to garnish

salt and pepper

350 g/12 oz dried fettuccine

cook's tip

Use saffron threads rather than ground saffron, as the powder may have been adulterated. Before cooking, discard any mussels with broken shells or any that refuse to close when tapped with a knife.

1 Place the saffron in a small bowl, add the hot water and leave to soak. Place the mussels in a large heavy-based saucepan. Add the cold water, cover and cook over a high heat, shaking the saucepan occasionally, for 5 minutes, or until the shells have opened. Remove the mussels with a slotted spoon, reserving the liquid. Discard any that have not opened and remove the remainder from their shells. Sieve the cooking liquid through a muslin-lined sieve and reserve.

2 Heat the oil in a frying pan. Add the onion and cook over a low heat, stirring, for 5 minutes, or until softened. Sprinkle in the flour and cook, stirring, for 1 minute. Remove the pan from the heat. Mix the vermouth and saffron liquid together and gradually whisk in to the frying pan. Return to the heat and simmer, stirring, for 2–3 minutes, or until thickened. Stir in 4 tablespoons of the reserved cooking liquid, the cheese, mussels and chives and season to taste with salt and pepper. Simmer for 4 minutes, or until heated through.

3 Meanwhile, bring a large heavy-based saucepan of lightly salted water to the boil. Add the pasta, return to the boil and cook for 8–10 minutes, or until tender but still firm to the bite. Drain and transfer to a large, warmed serving dish. Add the mussels and sauce, toss well, garnish with extra snipped chives and serve immediately.

linguine with clams in tomato sauce

⏱ **cook: 35 mins**　　　⏱ **prep: 20 mins**　　　　**serves 4**

NUTRITIONAL INFORMATION

Calories 476

Protein 24g

Carbohydrate 72g

Sugars 9g

Fat 8g

Saturates 1g

variation

Substitute the parsley with the same amount of shredded basil, and if you prefer a less spicy sauce, omit the chilli in Step 2.

Pasta eaters argue passionately about the right way to serve clams with pasta. Some are adherents to the classic Spaghetti con Vongole (see page 122) and are horrified by the combination with tomatoes and cheese, while others love this typically Neapolitan recipe. Actually, both are wonderful.

INGREDIENTS

225 ml/8 fl oz dry white wine

2 garlic cloves, roughly chopped

4 tbsp fresh flat-leaved parsley, roughly chopped

1 kg/2 lb 4 oz live clams, scrubbed

2 tbsp olive oil

1 onion, chopped

8 plum tomatoes, peeled, deseeded and chopped

1 fresh red chilli, deseeded and chopped

salt and pepper

350 g/12 oz dried linguine

cook's tip

Before cooking, discard any clams with damaged or broken shells and any that refuse to close when sharply tapped with a knife.

1 Pour the wine into a large heavy-based saucepan and add the garlic, half the parsley and the clams. Cover and cook over a high heat, shaking the saucepan occasionally, for 5 minutes, or until the shells have opened. Remove the clams with a slotted spoon, reserving the cooking liquid. Discard any that have not opened and remove half of the remainder from their shells. Keep the shelled and unshelled clams in separate covered bowls. Sieve the cooking liquid through a muslin-lined sieve and reserve.

2 Heat the olive oil in a heavy-based saucepan. Add the onion and cook over a low heat for 5 minutes, or until softened. Add the tomatoes, chilli and reserved cooking liquid and season to taste with salt and pepper. Bring to the boil, partially cover the saucepan and simmer for 20 minutes.

3 Meanwhile, bring a large heavy-based saucepan of lightly salted water to the boil. Add the pasta, return to the boil and cook for 8–10 minutes, or until tender but still firm to the bite. Drain and transfer to a warmed serving dish.

4 Stir the shelled clams into the tomato sauce and heat through gently for 2–3 minutes. Pour over the pasta and toss. Garnish with the clams in their shells and remaining parsley. Serve.

spaghetti con vongole

serves 4   **prep: 15 mins**   **cook: 15 mins**

This is the purist's classic combination of clams and pasta, cooked simply in white wine and flavoured with fresh parsley.

INGREDIENTS

1 kg/2 lb 4 oz live clams, scrubbed

175 ml/6 fl oz water

175 ml/6 fl oz dry white wine

350 g/12 oz dried spaghetti

5 tbsp olive oil

2 garlic cloves, finely chopped

4 tbsp chopped fresh

flat-leaved parsley

salt and pepper

NUTRITIONAL INFORMATION

Calories 512

Protein 23g

Carbohydrate 67g

Sugars 3g

Fat 16g

Saturates 2g

variation

If fresh clams are not available, use 2 x 400 g/14 oz jars of clams. Drain and rinse before adding to the frying pan in Step 3.

cook's tip

Shellfish, such as mussels and clams, are always sold alive. To test if they are alive, tap the shell gently and if it closes immediately, then it is alive. If not, it is dead, and should not be cooked or eaten.

1 Place the clams in a large heavy-based saucepan. Add the water and wine, then cover and cook over a high heat, shaking the saucepan occasionally, for 5 minutes, or until the shells have opened. Remove the clams with a slotted spoon and sieve the liquid through a muslin-lined sieve into a small saucepan. Bring to the boil and

cook until reduced by about half. Discard any clams that have not opened and remove the remainder from their shells.

2 Bring a large heavy-based saucepan of lightly salted water to the boil. Add the pasta, return to the boil and cook for 8–10 minutes, or until tender but still firm to the bite.

3 Meanwhile, heat the olive oil in a large heavy-based frying pan. Add the garlic and cook, stirring frequently, for 2 minutes. Add the parsley and the reduced cooking liquid and simmer gently. Drain the pasta and add it to the frying pan with the clams. Season to taste with salt and pepper and cook, stirring constantly, for

4 minutes, or until the pasta is coated and the clams have heated through. Transfer to a warmed serving dish and serve immediately.

pasta omelette with prawns

🕐 **cook: 20 mins**　　　🕐 **prep: 15 mins**　　　**serves 4**

variation

Substitute the dried spaghetti with dried vermicelli or bucatini and replace the pecorino cheese with the same amount of Parmesan cheese.

This different approach to serving pasta provides an easy, nourishing midweek family supper with very little to clear up afterwards. A salad of mixed leaves is the perfect complement.

INGREDIENTS

350 g/12 oz dried spaghetti

3 eggs

3 tbsp finely chopped fresh parsley

85 g/3 oz freshly grated pecorino cheese

225 g/8 oz cooked peeled prawns, deveined

salt and pepper

4 tbsp olive oil

whole cooked prawns, to garnish

mixed salad leaves, to serve

cook's tip

To speed up the cooking process, gently stir the egg and pasta mixture from the edge of the frying pan into the centre once the base has lightly set.

1 Bring a large heavy-based saucepan of lightly salted water to the boil. Add the pasta, return to the boil and cook for 8–10 minutes, or until tender but still firm to the bite. Drain well, then rinse under cold running water and drain again. Reserve until required.

2 Beat the eggs with the parsley and cheese, then stir in the prawns. Season to taste with salt and pepper and stir in the pasta.

3 Heat half the olive oil in a heavy-based frying pan. Pour in the egg and pasta mixture, tilt the frying pan to spread it evenly and cook over a medium heat, shaking the frying pan occasionally, until the top of the omelette is beginning to set and the underside is golden. Place a plate over the frying pan and invert the two. Heat the remaining oil in the frying pan, then slide the omelette back into the pan to cook the other side. Cut the omelette into wedges and transfer to warmed serving plates. Garnish with a few whole prawns and serve immediately with mixed salad leaves.

prawns, peas & pasta

serves 4   **prep: 15 mins** ⏱   **cook: 20 mins** ⏱

This pretty pink and green dish would be a good choice for a summery supper, served with a glass of chilled white wine.

INGREDIENTS

pinch of saffron threads

225 ml/8 fl oz dry white wine

3 tbsp olive oil

25 g/1 oz unsalted butter

1 shallot, chopped

225 g/8 oz peas

350 g/12 oz cooked peeled prawns

350 g/12 oz dried fusilli bucati or ditali

salt and pepper

2 tbsp snipped fresh dill, to garnish

NUTRITIONAL INFORMATION

Calories	.590
Protein	.34g
Carbohydrate	.71g
Sugars	.5g
Fat	.17g
Saturates	.5g

cook's tip

If you are using frozen cooked prawns and/or frozen peas, make sure that they are thoroughly thawed before you begin cooking this recipe.

1 Place the saffron in a small bowl, add the wine and leave to soak. Heat the olive oil and butter in a large heavy-based frying pan. Add the shallot and cook over a low heat, stirring occasionally, for 5 minutes, or until softened. Add the peas and cooked prawns and cook, stirring occasionally, for 2–3 minutes.

2 Bring a large heavy-based saucepan of lightly salted water to the boil. Add the pasta, return to the boil and cook for 8–10 minutes, or until tender but still firm to the bite.

3 Meanwhile, stir the saffron and wine mixture into the frying pan. Increase the heat and cook until the liquid is reduced by about half. Season to taste with salt and pepper. Drain the pasta and add to the frying pan. Cook for 1–2 minutes, or until it is well coated with the sauce. Transfer to a warmed serving dish, sprinkle with dill and serve immediately.

spaghetti with prawns & caviar

⏲ **cook: 12 mins**   ⏱ **prep: 10 mins**   **serves 4**

Expensive and wonderfully over the top, this sophisticated dish with the luxurious taste of caviar is strictly for adults.

NUTRITIONAL INFORMATION

Calories 720

Protein 27g

Carbohydrate 66g

Sugars 4g

Fat 33g

Saturates 13g

INGREDIENTS

350 g/12 oz dried spaghetti

4 tbsp olive oil

3 spring onions, thinly sliced

1 garlic clove, finely chopped

225 g/8 oz cooked peeled prawns, deveined, tails left on

125 ml/4 fl oz lemon-flavoured vodka

150 ml/5 fl oz double cream or panna da cucina

8 tbsp caviar, plus extra to garnish

salt and pepper

fresh chives, to garnish

cook's tip

Genuine caviar is expensive and, as the sturgeon from which it comes is quite rare, prices are climbing. Pressed caviar, made from damaged eggs, is cheaper.

1 Bring a large heavy-based saucepan of lightly salted water to the boil. Add the pasta, return to the boil and cook for 8–10 minutes, or until tender but still firm to the bite.

2 Meanwhile, heat the olive oil in a heavy-based frying pan. Add the spring onions and the garlic and cook over a low heat, stirring occasionally, for 3–4 minutes, or until softened. Add the prawns and cook, stirring occasionally, for 2 minutes. Pour in the vodka and cream and simmer gently for 5 minutes. Remove the frying pan from the heat. With a slotted spoon, remove the prawns from the sauce and reserve.

3 Stir the caviar into the cream sauce and season to taste with salt and pepper. Drain the pasta and tip it into the sauce. Toss to coat and transfer to warmed serving plates. Garnish with the prawns, extra caviar and chives and serve immediately.

linguine with prawns & scallops

serves 6   **prep: 15 mins**   **cook: 30 mins**

Using the prawn shells to flavour the sauce – they are discarded before serving – gives a subtle depth to this fabulous dish.

INGREDIENTS

450 g/1 lb raw prawns

25 g/1 oz butter

2 shallots, finely chopped

225 ml/8 fl oz dry white vermouth

350 ml/12 fl oz water

450 g/1 lb dried linguine

2 tbsp olive oil

450 g/1 lb prepared scallops, thawed if frozen

2 tbsp snipped fresh chives

salt and pepper

NUTRITIONAL INFORMATION

Calories	.487
Protein	.33g
Carbohydrate	.61g
Sugars	.5g
Fat	.10g
Saturates	.3g

cook's tip

Both scallops and prawns become tough when over-cooked, so keep stirring and do not cook for longer than necessary in Step 3.

1 Peel and devein the prawns, reserving the shells. Melt the butter in a heavy-based frying pan. Add the shallots and cook over a low heat, stirring occasionally, for 5 minutes, or until softened. Add the prawn shells and cook, stirring constantly, for 1 minute. Pour in the vermouth and cook, stirring, for 1 minute. Add the water, bring to the boil, then

reduce the heat and simmer for 10 minutes, or until the liquid has reduced by half. Remove the frying pan from the heat.

2 Bring a large heavy-based saucepan of lightly salted water to the boil. Add the pasta, return to the boil and cook for 8–10 minutes, or until tender but still firm to the bite.

3 Meanwhile, heat the oil in a separate heavy-based frying pan. Add the scallops and prawns and cook, stirring frequently, for 2 minutes, or until the scallops are opaque and the prawns have changed colour. Sieve the prawn-shell stock into the frying pan. Drain the pasta and add to the frying pan with the chives and season to taste

with salt and pepper. Toss well over a low heat for 1 minute, then serve.

scallops with black tagliatelle

⏱ **cook: 12–15 mins**   ⏱ **prep: 15 mins**   **serves 4**

Serving this dramatic looking dish is sure to impress your guests – nor will they be disappointed when they taste it.

NUTRITIONAL INFORMATION	
Calories	.690
Protein	.32g
Carbohydrate	.75g
Sugars	.9g
Fat	.29g
Saturates	.13g

INGREDIENTS

350 g/12 oz prepared scallops, thawed if frozen

3 tbsp olive oil

1 onion, finely chopped

1 garlic clove, finely chopped

2 carrots, cut into thin batons

350 g/12 oz black tagliatelle

2 tbsp dry white wine

2 tbsp anise, such as Pernod

1 tbsp snipped fresh dill

150 ml/5 fl oz double cream or panna da cucina

salt and pepper

cook's tip

To prepare a scallop, hold the shell flat-side up, insert a knife blade to cut the top muscle, then separate the shells. Slide the blade under the 'skirt' to cut the lower muscle. Remove the white muscle and coral.

1 Separate the corals from the scallops, if necessary, and cut the white muscle in half. Heat the olive oil in a frying pan. Add the onion, garlic and carrots and cook over a low heat for 8 minutes, or until softened.

2 Meanwhile, bring a large heavy-based saucepan of lightly salted water to the boil. Add the pasta, return to the boil and cook for 8–10 minutes, or until tender but still firm to the bite.

3 Add the scallops with any corals, wine, anise and dill to the frying pan. Cover and simmer for 1 minute. With a slotted spoon, transfer the scallops, corals and vegetables to a large heatproof plate, then cover and keep warm. Bring the cooking juices to the boil and cook until reduced by about half, then stir in the cream.

4 Return the scallops, corals and vegetables to the frying pan, season to taste with salt and pepper and heat through gently. Drain the pasta and transfer to a warmed serving dish. Pour the scallops and their sauce over the pasta, toss well and serve immediately.

cavatappi with squid in fennel sauce

serves 4   **prep: 15 mins**   **cook: 30 mins**

A delicious combination of squid and fennel is perfect for any special occasion. Serve with mixed salad leaves and crusty bread.

INGREDIENTS

1 tbsp olive oil

350 g/12 oz prepared squid,
sliced into rings (see Cook's Tip)

4 tbsp anise, such as Pernod

400 g/14 oz canned chopped tomatoes

1 fennel bulb, grated

2 shallots, finely chopped

350 g/12 oz dried cavatappi

salt and pepper

NUTRITIONAL INFORMATION	
Calories	.446
Protein	.25g
Carbohydrate	.70g
Sugars	.7g
Fat	.5g
Saturates	.1g

cook's tip

To prepare squid, pull the head from the body. Cut off the tentacles and squeeze out the beak. Remove and discard the 'quill' from the body sac. Rinse the sac under cold running water and rub off the skin.

1 Heat the olive oil in a heavy-based frying pan. Add the squid and cook, stirring frequently, for 2 minutes. Add the anise and cook for 1 minute, then transfer the squid to a plate with a slotted spoon. Add the tomatoes, fennel and shallots to the frying pan, cover and simmer, stirring occasionally, for 20 minutes, or until thickened.

2 Meanwhile, bring a large heavy-based saucepan of lightly salted water to the boil. Add the pasta, return to the boil and cook for 8–10 minutes, or until tender but still firm to the bite.

3 Return the squid to the frying pan, season to taste with salt and pepper and heat through gently for 2 minutes. Drain the pasta and transfer to a warmed bowl. Spoon the squid sauce over the pasta, toss well and serve immediately.

penne with squid & tomatoes

⏲ **cook: 25 mins**   ⏱ **prep: 15 mins**   **serves 4**

All the ingredients, including the pasta, cook together in a single saucepan for an easy dish and a delicious melding of flavours.

NUTRITIONAL INFORMATION	
Calories	.485
Protein	.23g
Carbohydrate	.53g
Sugars	.11g
Fat	.19g
Saturates	.2g

INGREDIENTS

225 g/8 oz dried penne

350 g/12 oz prepared squid
(see Cook's Tip, page 130)

6 tbsp olive oil

2 onions, sliced

225 ml/8 fl oz Fish or Chicken Stock
(see page 12)

150 ml/5 fl oz full-bodied red wine

400 g/14 oz canned chopped tomatoes

2 tbsp tomato purée

1 tbsp chopped fresh marjoram

1 bay leaf

salt and pepper

2 tbsp chopped fresh parsley

1 Bring a large heavy-based saucepan of lightly salted water to the boil. Add the pasta, return to the boil and cook for 3 minutes, then drain and reserve until required. With a sharp knife, cut the squid into strips.

2 Heat the olive oil in a large flameproof dish or casserole. Add the onions and cook over a low heat, stirring occasionally, for 5 minutes, or until softened. Add the squid and Fish Stock, bring to the boil and simmer for 3 minutes. Stir in the wine, chopped tomatoes and their can juices, tomato purée, marjoram and bay leaf. Season to taste with salt and pepper. Bring to the boil and cook for 5 minutes, or until slightly reduced.

3 Add the pasta, return to the boil and simmer for 5–7 minutes, or until tender but still firm to the bite. Remove and discard the bay leaf, stir in the parsley and serve immediately, straight from the dish.

cook's tip

The sauce should be quite thick. If it seems too liquid by the time the pasta is tender, boil vigorously for a couple of minutes to reduce.

vegetables & salads

As a combination of pasta and vegetables is both appetising and attractive, it is a popular choice for everyone, not just vegetarians. Tomatoes, inevitably, take a starring role, and dishes such as Neapolitan Conchiglie (see page 134) and Tagliatelle with Sun-dried Tomatoes (see page 162) amply demonstrate why. The on-going Italian love affair with mushrooms is also apparent from such mouthwatering classics as Linguine with Wild Mushrooms (see page 163) and Penne with Creamy Mushrooms (see page 160). Pasta goes superbly with all the typical Mediterranean vegetables – aubergines, courgettes, fennel, pumpkin, olives, beans, peppers and artichokes – and these are featured in sauces and fillings on their own or mixed together in a melt-in-the-mouth medley.

There are dishes for all occasions, whether you are offering guests Saffron Tagliatelle with Asparagus (see page 142) or Casarecci with Artichokes (see page 148); or feeding a hungry family with Vegetable Lasagne (see page 154) or Penne with Mixed Beans (see page 164). Pasta salads are always popular and the perfect choice for entertaining, whether as part of a buffet table or to accompany a barbecue, especially as they can be made in advance. For family meals, they bring a welcome change from lettuce and tomatoes in the summer and a refreshing alternative when salad leaves are out of season in the winter. The recipes feature ingredients as diverse as pears, cheese, rocket, nuts, olives and curry powder, as once again pasta demonstrates its wonderful adaptability.

neapolitan conchiglie

serves 4   **prep: 15 mins**   **cook: 50 mins**

Naples' most famous daughter, film star Sophia Loren, once remarked that 'everything you see I owe to pasta'. When you have eaten this classic pasta in tomato sauce, get ready for your screen test!

INGREDIENTS

900 g/2 lb plum tomatoes, roughly chopped

150 ml/5 fl oz dry white wine

1 onion, chopped

1 carrot, chopped

1 celery stick, chopped

2 fresh flat-leaved parsley sprigs

pinch of sugar

salt

350 g/12 oz dried conchiglie

1 tbsp chopped fresh marjoram

freshly grated Parmesan cheese, to serve

NUTRITIONAL INFORMATION

Calories	385
Protein	13g
Carbohydrate	77g
Sugars	14g
Fat	3g
Saturates	0g

variation

Although fresh plum tomatoes are best for this recipe, you could use 800 g/1 lb 12 oz canned chopped plum tomatoes instead.

1 Place the tomatoes in a large heavy-based saucepan. Add the wine, onion, carrot, celery, parsley and sugar and gradually bring to the boil, stirring frequently. Reduce the heat, partially cover and simmer, stirring occasionally, for 45 minutes, or until thickened.

2 Meanwhile, bring a large heavy-based saucepan of lightly salted water to the boil. Add the pasta, return to the boil and cook for 8–10 minutes, or until tender but still firm to the bite.

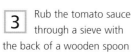

3 Rub the tomato sauce through a sieve with the back of a wooden spoon into a clean saucepan and stir in the marjoram. Reheat gently, stirring occasionally, for 1–2 minutes. Drain the pasta and transfer to a warmed serving dish. Pour the tomato sauce over the pasta and toss well. Sprinkle with Parmesan cheese and serve immediately with extra grated Parmesan cheese, if you like.

vermicelli with vegetable ribbons

⏱ **cook: 15 mins**　　　　⏳ **prep: 15 mins**　　　　**serves 4**

Colourful and tasty, this medley of pasta, vegetables and fresh herbs would make a wonderful family lunch on a busy Saturday. Serve with a salad of mixed leaves and crusty bread, if you like.

NUTRITIONAL INFORMATION	
Calories	414
Protein	13g
Carbohydrate	73g
Sugars	7g
Fat	10g
Saturates	4g

INGREDIENTS

350 g/12 oz dried vermicelli

3 courgettes

3 carrots

25 g/1 oz unsalted butter

1 tbsp olive oil

2 garlic cloves, finely chopped

85 g/3 oz fresh basil, shredded

25 g/1 oz fresh chives, finely snipped

25 g/1 oz fresh flat-leaved parsley, finely chopped

salt and pepper

1 small head radicchio, leaves shredded

variation

If you like, you can garnish the dish with thin shavings of Parmesan cheese or crumbled feta cheese.

1 Bring a large heavy-based saucepan of lightly salted water to the boil. Add the pasta, return to the boil and cook for 8–10 minutes, or until tender but still firm to the bite.

2 Meanwhile, cut the courgettes and carrots into very thin strips with a swivel-blade vegetable peeler or a mandolin. Melt the butter with the olive oil in a heavy-based frying pan. Add the carrot strips and garlic and cook over a low heat, stirring occasionally, for 5 minutes. Add the courgette strips and all the herbs and season to taste with salt and pepper.

3 Drain the pasta and add it to the frying pan. Toss well to mix and cook, stirring occasionally, for 5 minutes. Transfer to a warmed serving dish, add the radicchio, toss well and serve immediately.

mushroom cannelloni

serves 4   **prep: 25 mins**   **cook: 40 mins**

Wild mushrooms have a rich, earthy flavour that is perfect for this filled pasta dish, but you could use a more economical mixture of wild and cultivated mushrooms, if you like.

INGREDIENTS

12 dried cannelloni tubes

4 tbsp olive oil, plus extra
for brushing

25 g/1 oz butter

450 g/1 lb mixed wild mushrooms,
finely chopped

1 garlic clove, finely chopped

85 g/3 oz fresh breadcrumbs

150 ml/5 fl oz milk

225 g/8 oz ricotta cheese

6 tbsp freshly grated Parmesan cheese

salt and pepper

2 tbsp pine kernels

2 tbsp flaked almonds

TOMATO SAUCE

2 tbsp olive oil

1 onion, finely chopped

1 garlic clove, finely chopped

800 g/1 lb 12 oz canned
chopped tomatoes

1 tbsp tomato purée

8 black olives, stoned and chopped

salt and pepper

NUTRITIONAL INFORMATION

Calories 727

Protein 26g

Carbohydrate 59g

Sugars 14g

Fat 44g

Saturates 15g

variation

Substitute half the quantity of wild mushrooms with exotic cultivated mushrooms, such as shiitake, and ordinary mushrooms, such as buttons.

cook's tip

Use either a teaspoon or a piping bag fitted with a large plain nozzle to fill the canelloni tubes. Do not overfill them.

1 Preheat the oven to 190°C/375°F/Gas Mark 5. Bring a large saucepan of lightly salted water to the boil. Add the cannelloni tubes, return to the boil and cook for 8–10 minutes, or until tender but still firm to the bite. With a slotted spoon, transfer the cannelloni tubes to a plate and pat dry. Brush a large ovenproof dish with olive oil.

2 Meanwhile, make the tomato sauce. Heat the olive oil in a frying pan. Add the onion and garlic and cook over a low heat for 5 minutes, or until softened. Add the tomatoes and their can juices, tomato purée and olives and season to taste with salt and pepper. Bring to the boil and cook for 3–4 minutes. Pour the sauce into the ovenproof dish.

3 To make the filling, melt the butter in a heavy-based frying pan. Add the mushrooms and garlic and cook over a medium heat, stirring frequently, for 3–5 minutes, or until tender. Remove the frying pan from the heat. Mix the breadcrumbs, milk and oil together in a large bowl, then stir in the ricotta, mushroom mixture and 4 tablespoons of the Parmesan cheese. Season to taste with salt and pepper.

4 Fill the cannelloni tubes with the mushroom mixture and place them in the dish. Brush with olive oil and sprinkle with the remaining Parmesan cheese, pine kernels and almonds. Bake in the oven for 25 minutes, or until golden.

pappardelle with pumpkin sauce

⏱ **cook: 1 hr 15 mins**   ⏱ **prep: 15 mins**   **serves 4**

NUTRITIONAL INFORMATION

Calories 580

Protein 18g

Carbohydrate 74g

Sugars 10g

Fat 26g

Saturates 16g

variation

If pumpkins are not available, then use other types of squash, such as butternut or acorn squash, instead.

Slow cooking is the key to success with this classic, rich pumpkin sauce which captures the special warmth of the Campania region of southern Italy.

INGREDIENTS

55 g/2 oz butter

6 shallots, very finely chopped

salt

800 g/1 lb 12 oz pumpkin, peeled, deseeded and cut into pieces

pinch of freshly grated nutmeg

200 ml/7 fl oz single cream

4 tbsp freshly grated Parmesan cheese, plus extra to serve

2 tbsp chopped fresh flat-leaved parsley

350 g/12 oz dried pappardelle

cook's tip

To prepare the pumpkin, use a sharp knife to cut it into quarters. Scrape the seeds out with a dessertspoon and discard, then peel and cut the flesh into batons.

1 Melt the butter in a large heavy-based saucepan. Add the shallots, sprinkle with a little salt, cover and cook over a very low heat, stirring occasionally, for 30 minutes.

2 Add the pumpkin pieces and season to taste with nutmeg. Cover and cook over a very low heat,

stirring occasionally, for 40 minutes, or until the pumpkin is pulpy. Stir in the cream, Parmesan cheese and parsley and remove the saucepan from the heat.

3 Meanwhile, bring a large heavy-based saucepan of lightly salted water to the boil. Add the pasta, return to the boil and

cook for 8–10 minutes, or until tender but still firm to the bite. Drain, reserving 2–3 tablespoons of the cooking water.

4 Add the pasta to the pumpkin mixture and stir in the reserved cooking water if the mixture seems too thick. Cook, stirring, for 1 minute, then transfer to a

warmed serving dish and serve immediately with extra grated Parmesan cheese.

fettuccine with peppers roman style

serves 4   **prep: 15 mins**   **cook: 40 mins**

Red, yellow or orange peppers are all suitable for this dish, but green peppers are a little too sharp in taste and do not provide enough contrast with the saltiness of the olives.

INGREDIENTS

100 ml/3½ fl oz olive oil

1 onion, finely chopped

200 g/7 oz black olives, stoned and roughly chopped

400 g/14 oz canned chopped tomatoes, drained

2 red, yellow or orange peppers, deseeded and cut into thin strips

salt and pepper

350 g/12 oz dried fettuccine

freshly grated pecorino cheese, to serve

NUTRITIONAL INFORMATION	
Calories	.555
Protein	.13g
Carbohydrate	.72g
Sugars	.9g
Fat	.26g
Saturates	.4g

cook's tip

Traditionally, tiny black wrinkled olives grown in the Lazio region of Italy are used for this Roman dish, but you could use Spanish or even Greek Kalamata olives, if you like.

1 Heat the olive oil in a large heavy-based saucepan. Add the onion and cook over a low heat, stirring occasionally, for 5 minutes, or until softened. Add the olives, tomatoes and peppers and season to taste with salt and pepper. Cover and simmer gently over a very low heat, stirring occasionally, for 35 minutes.

2 Meanwhile, bring a large heavy-based saucepan of lightly salted water to the boil. Add the pasta, return to the boil and cook for 8–10 minutes, or until tender but still firm to the bite. Drain the pasta and transfer to a warmed serving dish.

3 Spoon the sauce on to the pasta and toss well. Sprinkle generously with the pecorino cheese and serve immediately, with extra grated pecorino cheese.

farfalle with aubergines

cook: 45 mins   **prep: 15 mins**   **serves 4**

This classic combination of aubergines, tomatoes, pasta and lots of fresh basil is ideal for a quick summer lunch. Any type of short pasta would be suitable for this dish, such as penne or conchiglie.

NUTRITIONAL INFORMATION

Calories 584

Protein 12g

Carbohydrate 72g

Sugars 9g

Fat 30g

Saturates 4g

INGREDIENTS

1 large or 2 medium aubergines, diced

salt and pepper

150 ml/5 fl oz olive oil

4 shallots, chopped

2 garlic cloves, finely chopped

400 g/14 oz canned chopped tomatoes

1 tsp caster sugar

350 g/12 oz dried farfalle

fresh basil sprigs, to garnish

cook's tip

While there is no longer the need to salt modern varieties of aubergines to absorb bitter juices, it is still worth doing because it prevents them from absorbing a lot of oil during frying.

1 Place the aubergine in a colander, sprinkling each layer with salt, and leave to drain for 30 minutes. Meanwhile, heat 1 tablespoon of the olive oil in a heavy-based saucepan. Add the shallots and garlic and cook over a low heat, stirring occasionally, for 5 minutes, or until softened. Add the tomatoes and their can juices,

stir in the sugar and season to taste with salt and pepper. Cover and simmer gently, stirring occasionally, for 30 minutes, or until thickened.

2 Rinse the aubergine under cold running water, drain well and pat dry with kitchen paper. Heat half the remaining olive oil in a heavy-based frying pan, then

add the aubergine in batches, and cook, stirring frequently, until golden brown all over. Remove from the frying pan with a slotted spoon and keep warm while you cook the remaining batches, adding the remaining oil as necessary.

3 Meanwhile, bring a large heavy-based saucepan of lightly salted

water to the boil. Add the pasta, return to the boil and cook for 8–10 minutes, or until tender but still firm to the bite. Drain the pasta and transfer to a warmed serving dish.

4 Pour the tomato sauce over the pasta and toss well to mix. Top with the diced aubergine, garnish with fresh basil sprigs and serve.

saffron tagliatelle with asparagus

serves 4   **prep: 15 mins**   **cook: 20 mins**

The easy option of serving pasta to vegetarian guests has become something of a cliché, but this is so special that an exception must be made. Cooking the pasta in the same water as the asparagus intensifies the flavour.

INGREDIENTS

pinch of saffron threads	grated rind and juice of ½ lemon
2 tbsp hot water	salt and pepper
450 g/1 lb asparagus spears	115 g/4 oz shelled fresh peas
25 g/1 oz butter	350 g/12 oz dried tagliatelle
1 small onion, finely chopped	2 tbsp chopped fresh chervil
2 tbsp dry white wine	fresh Parmesan cheese shavings
225 ml/8 fl oz double cream or	
panna da cucina	

NUTRITIONAL INFORMATION

Calories 656

Protein 17g

Carbohydrate 73g

Sugars 8g

Fat 35g

Saturates 20g

variation

Substitute the chopped fresh chervil with the same amount of shredded fresh basil and use frozen peas if fresh ones are not available.

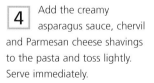

cook's tip

To make shavings of fresh Parmesan cheese, hold the block of cheese in one hand and use a vegetable peeler to pare off small pieces or shavings into a bowl or over the finished dish.

1 Place the saffron in a small bowl, stir in the hot water and leave to soak. Trim off and reserve 5 cm/ 2 inches of the asparagus tips and slice the remainder.

2 Melt the butter in a heavy-based saucepan. Add the onion and cook over a low heat, stirring occasionally, for 5 minutes, or until softened. Add the wine, cream and saffron mixture. Bring to the boil, stirring constantly, then reduce the heat and simmer for 5 minutes, or until slightly thickened. Stir in the lemon rind and juice and season with salt and pepper.

3 Meanwhile, bring a large heavy-based saucepan of lightly salted water to the boil. Add the reserved asparagus tips and cook for 1 minute. Remove with a slotted spoon and add to the cream sauce. Cook the peas and sliced asparagus in the boiling water for 8 minutes, or until tender. With a slotted spoon, transfer them to the cream sauce. Add the pasta to the water, return to the boil and cook for 8–10 minutes, or until tender but still firm to the bite. Drain the pasta and transfer to a warmed serving dish.

4 Add the creamy asparagus sauce, chervil and Parmesan cheese shavings to the pasta and toss lightly. Serve immediately.

pappardelle with asparagus

serves 4   **prep: 15 mins**   **cook: 35 mins**

The first young vegetables of the summer are always a welcome sight. Make the most of them while they are in season.

INGREDIENTS

750 g/1 lb 10 oz asparagus spears

85 g/3 oz butter

1 onion, chopped

2 carrots, chopped

1 celery stick, chopped

400 g/14 oz canned chopped tomatoes, drained (see Cook's Tip)

salt and pepper

350 g/12 oz dried pappardelle

freshly grated Parmesan cheese, to serve

NUTRITIONAL INFORMATION

Calories	.537
Protein	.18g
Carbohydrate	.76g
Sugars	.13g
Fat	.20g
Saturates	.12g

cook's tip

Reserve the can juices when you drain the tomatoes. If the mixture seems to be drying out while simmering in Step 2, add a little of the reserved juice.

1 With a sharp knife, trim off and reserve about 5 cm/2 inches of the asparagus tips and cut the remainder into 4-cm/1½-inch chunks. Melt the butter in a large heavy-based saucepan. Add the onion, carrots and celery and cook over a low heat, stirring occasionally, for 10 minutes or until the vegetables are softened.

2 Add all the asparagus and cook over a low heat for 5 minutes. Add the tomatoes and season to taste with salt and pepper. Cover and simmer for 20 minutes.

3 Meanwhile, bring a large heavy-based saucepan of lightly salted water to the boil. Add the pasta, return to the boil and cook for 8–10 minutes, or until tender but still firm to the bite. Drain the pasta and transfer to a warmed serving dish. Spoon the asparagus sauce on to it and toss lightly. Sprinkle with Parmesan cheese and serve immediately.

spaghettini with tomatoes & black olives

⏲ **cook: 30 mins**   ⏱ **prep: 15 mins**   **serves 4**

This sauce is reminiscent of the classic pizza combination –
tomatoes, olives and capers – with dried chilli to add extra interest.

NUTRITIONAL INFORMATION

Calories 307

Protein 11g

Carbohydrate 51g

Sugars 11g

Fat 8g

Saturates 2g

INGREDIENTS

1 tbsp olive oil

1 garlic clove, finely chopped

2 tsp bottled capers, drained,
rinsed and chopped

12 black olives, stoned and chopped

½ dried red chilli, crushed

1.25 kg/2 lb 12 oz canned tomatoes

salt

1 tbsp chopped fresh parsley, plus
extra to garnish

350 g/12 oz dried spaghettini

2 tbsp freshly grated Parmesan cheese

mixed salad, to serve

cook's tip

Capers are the flower buds of a Mediterranean bush. They are preserved in a mixture of vinegar and salt or in salt alone and should be rinsed before use. Sometimes they are available preserved in olive oil.

1 Heat the olive oil in a large heavy-based frying pan. Add the garlic and cook over a low heat for 30 seconds, then add the capers, olives, dried chilli and tomatoes and season to taste with salt. Partially cover the pan and simmer gently for 20 minutes.

2 Stir in the parsley, partially cover the frying pan again and simmer for a further 10 minutes.

3 Meanwhile, bring a large heavy-based saucepan of lightly salted water to the boil. Add the pasta, return to the boil and cook for 8–10 minutes, or until tender but still firm to the bite. Drain and transfer to a warmed serving dish. Add the tomato and olive sauce and toss well. Sprinkle the Parmesan over the pasta and garnish with extra chopped parsley. Serve immediately with a mixed salad.

cannelloni in tomato & red pepper sauce

cook: 50 mins **prep: 25 mins** **serves 4**

NUTRITIONAL INFORMATION

Calories 822

Protein 23g

Carbohydrate 65g

Sugars 20g

Fat 54g

Saturates 24g

variation

Replace the grated pecorino cheese with the same amount of freshly grated Parmesan cheese. You can use either white or wholemeal breadcrumbs.

The creamy mascarpone and broccoli filling really does melt in the mouth when you bite into these delicious cannelloni.

INGREDIENTS

12 dried cannelloni tubes

4 tbsp olive oil, plus extra for brushing

450 g/1 lb broccoli, broken into florets

85 g/3 oz fresh breadcrumbs

150 ml/5 fl oz milk

225 g/8 oz mascarpone cheese

pinch of grated nutmeg

6 tbsp freshly grated pecorino cheese

salt and pepper

2 tbsp flaked almonds

TOMATO & RED PEPPER SAUCE

2 tbsp olive oil

4 shallots, finely chopped

1 garlic clove, finely chopped

600 g/1 lb 5 oz plum tomatoes, skinned, deseeded and chopped

3 red peppers, deseeded and chopped

1 tbsp sun-dried tomato paste

salt and pepper

1 tbsp shredded basil leaves

cook's tip

To peel tomatoes, use a knife to make a cross in the skin of each tomato. Place in a bowl and pour over enough boiling water to cover and soak for 10 seconds. Drain and rinse, then peel off the skin.

1 Preheat the oven to 190°C/375°F/Gas Mark 5. Bring a large heavy-based saucepan of lightly salted water to the boil. Add the pasta, return to the boil and cook for 8–10 minutes, or until tender but still firm to the bite. Transfer the pasta to a plate and pat dry with kitchen paper. Brush a large ovenproof dish with olive oil.

2 Meanwhile, make the sauce. Heat the oil in a frying pan. Add the shallots and garlic and cook over a low heat for 5 minutes, or until softened. Add the tomatoes, peppers and sun-dried tomato paste and season with salt and pepper. Bring to the boil, then reduce the heat and simmer for 20 minutes. Stir in the basil and pour the sauce into the dish.

3 While the sauce is cooking, place the broccoli in a saucepan of lightly salted boiling water and cook for 10 minutes, or until tender. Drain and leave to cool slightly, then process to a purée in a food processor. Mix the breadcrumbs, milk and oil together in a large bowl, then stir in the mascarpone cheese, nutmeg, broccoli purée and

4 tablespoons of the pecorino cheese. Season to taste with salt and pepper.

4 Fill the cannelloni tubes with the broccoli mixture and place them in the dish. Brush with olive oil and sprinkle with the remaining pecorino cheese and almonds. Bake in the preheated oven for 25 minutes, or until golden.

casarecci with artichokes

serves 4　　　　**prep: 20 mins**　　　　**cook: 35 mins**

Globe artichokes are native to Italy and they still retain a special place in Italian cuisine. They are associated with many classic Roman dishes. Here they are combined with that other Italian favourite, fennel.

INGREDIENTS

2 tbsp lemon juice

2 globe artichokes

2 tbsp olive oil

1 onion, finely chopped

2 garlic cloves, finely chopped

1 fennel bulb, thinly sliced and

feathery fronds reserved

3 tbsp chopped fresh

flat-leaved parsley

150 ml/5 fl oz dry white wine

600 g/1 lb 5 oz plum tomatoes, peeled,

deseeded and chopped

salt and pepper

350 g/12 oz dried casarecci

freshly grated Parmesan cheese,

to serve (optional)

variation

If you cannot find gemelli, then use dried short-cut macaroni or penne rigate instead.

cook's tip

Acidulated water prevents the artichokes from discolouring. However, they can blacken your hands when you are preparing them. To prevent this, rub your hands with 2 tablespoons lemon juice before you begin.

1 Fill a bowl with cold water and add the lemon juice. Break off the artichoke stalks, then pull off and discard the outer leaves. Cut off the tops of the pale, inner leaves. Cut the bases in half lengthways and pull out and discard the choke. Thinly slice the artichokes lengthways, adding the slices to the acidulated water as you go.

2 Heat the olive oil in a large heavy-based frying pan. Add the chopped onion, garlic, fennel and parsley and cook over a low heat, stirring frequently, for 8–10 minutes. Pour in the white wine, add the chopped tomatoes and season to taste with salt and pepper. Cover and simmer gently for 15 minutes.

3 Meanwhile, bring a large saucepan of lightly salted water to the boil. Drain the artichokes, then add to the water and cook for 5 minutes. Drain and stir into the frying pan. Cover and cook for 10 minutes.

4 Bring a separate large heavy-based saucepan of lightly salted water to the

boil. Add the pasta, return to the boil and cook for 8–10 minutes, or until tender but still firm to the bite. Drain the pasta and transfer to a warmed serving dish. Add the artichoke sauce and toss. Garnish with the reserved fennel fronds and serve immediately with Parmesan cheese, if you like.

ziti with rocket

serves 4   **prep: 10 mins**   **cook: 12 mins**

Now a city restaurant favourite, this was once a peasant dish from Calabria, where rocket grows wild. It is traditionally made with ziti, wide pasta tubes, which may be smooth or ridged, but you could use elbow macaroni instead, if you like.

INGREDIENTS

350 g/12 oz dried ziti, broken into 4-cm/1½-inch lengths

5 tbsp extra virgin olive oil

2 garlic cloves, lightly crushed

200 g/7 oz rocket

2 fresh red chillies, thickly sliced

freshly grated pecorino cheese, to serve

NUTRITIONAL INFORMATION

Calories 439

Protein 12g

Carbohydrate 66g

Sugars 4g

Fat 16g

Saturates 2g

variation

Substitute the rocket with the same amount of baby spinach leaves and replace the pecorino with Parmesan.

cook's tip

Wild rocket has a more pungent, peppery flavour than the cultivated variety. However, if you find it is too strong, blanch the leaves for 1 minute in boiling water and pat dry before stir-frying.

1 Bring a large heavy-based saucepan of lightly salted water to the boil. Add the pasta, return to the boil and cook for 8–10 minutes, or until tender but still firm to the bite.

2 Meanwhile, heat the olive oil in a large heavy-based frying pan. Add the garlic, rocket and chillies and stir-fry for 5 minutes, or until the rocket has wilted.

3 Stir 2 tablespoons of the pasta cooking water into the rocket, then drain the pasta and add to the frying pan. Cook, stirring frequently, for 2 minutes, then transfer to a warmed serving dish. Remove and discard the garlic cloves and chillies and serve immediately with the pecorino cheese.

macaroni with roasted vegetables

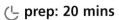

⏱ **cook: 40 mins**   ⏱ **prep: 20 mins**   **serves 4**

Roasting Mediterranean vegetables brings out their sweetness and full flavour to make a naturally rich sauce for pasta.

INGREDIENTS

2 onions, cut into wedges

2 courgettes, cut into chunks

1 red pepper, deseeded and cut into chunks

1 yellow pepper, deseeded and cut into chunks

1 aubergine cut into chunks

450 g/1 lb plum tomatoes, quartered and deseeded

3 garlic cloves, chopped

4 tbsp olive oil

salt and pepper

350 g/12 oz dried short-cut macaroni

300 ml/10 fl oz passata

85 g/3 oz black olives, stoned and halved

TO GARNISH

fresh basil sprigs

fresh flat-leaved parsley sprigs

variation

Other vegetables would work well in this dish, such as red onions, bite-sized pieces of butternut squash and cherry tomato halves.

cook's tip

When buying fresh tomatoes, always choose ones that are firm and bright red. Ripe tomatoes can be stored in the refrigerator for up to 2 days, and underripe ones should be kept at room temperature.

1 Preheat the oven to 240°C/475°F/Gas Mark 9. Spread out the onions, courgettes, red and yellow peppers, aubergine and tomatoes in a single layer in a large roasting tin. Sprinkle with the garlic, drizzle with the olive oil and season to taste with salt and pepper. Stir well until all the vegetables are coated. Roast in the preheated oven

for 15 minutes, then remove from the oven and stir well. Return to the oven for a further 15 minutes.

2 Bring a large heavy-based saucepan of lightly salted water to the boil. Add the pasta, return to the boil and cook for 8–10 minutes, or until tender but still firm to the bite.

3 Meanwhile, transfer the roasted vegetables to a large heavy-based saucepan and add the passata and olives. Heat through gently, stirring occasionally. Drain the pasta and transfer to a warmed serving dish. Add the roasted vegetable sauce and toss well. Garnish with the fresh basil and parsley and serve immediately.

vegetable lasagne

cook: 45–55 mins   **prep: 25 mins**   **serves 4**

NUTRITIONAL INFORMATION	
Calories	.930
Protein	.35g
Carbohydrate	.60g
Sugars	.18g
Fat	.62g
Saturates	.28g

variation

Replace the courgettes with 4 red peppers, cut into strips and cooked in the griddle pan. Substitute the plain lasagne with spinach-flavoured lasagne.

Layers of pasta, Mediterranean vegetables, mozzarella cheese and a creamy sauce would make a substantial and delicious vegetarian main dish at any time of year.

INGREDIENTS

olive oil, for brushing

2 aubergines, sliced

25 g/1 oz butter

1 garlic clove, finely chopped

4 courgettes, sliced

1 tbsp finely chopped fresh

flat-leaved parsley

1 tbsp finely chopped fresh marjoram

225 g/8 oz mozzarella cheese, grated

600 ml/1 pint passata

175 g/6 oz dried no-pre-cook lasagne

salt and pepper

600 ml/1 pint Béchamel Sauce

(see page 12)

55 g/2 oz freshly grated

Parmesan cheese

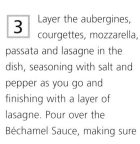

cook's tip

Make sure that the oiled griddle pan is very hot before adding the aubergine slices. Add extra oil if the aubergines are sticking to the pan.

1 Preheat the oven to 200°C/400°F/Gas Mark 6. Brush a large ovenproof dish with olive oil. Brush a large griddle pan with olive oil and heat until smoking. Add half the aubergines and cook over a medium heat for 8 minutes, or until golden brown all over. Remove from the griddle pan and drain on kitchen paper.

Add the remaining aubergine slices and extra oil, if necessary, and cook for 8 minutes, or until golden brown all over.

2 Melt the butter in a frying pan and add the garlic, courgettes, parsley and marjoram. Cook over a medium heat, stirring frequently, for 5 minutes, or until the courgettes are golden brown all

over. Remove from the frying pan and leave to drain on kitchen paper.

3 Layer the aubergines, courgettes, mozzarella, passata and lasagne in the dish, seasoning with salt and pepper as you go and finishing with a layer of lasagne. Pour over the Béchamel Sauce, making sure

that all the pasta is covered. Sprinkle with the grated Parmesan cheese and bake in the preheated oven for 30–40 minutes, or until golden brown. Serve immediately.

mixed vegetable agnolotti

serves 4   **prep: 25 mins** ⟳   **cook: 45–50 mins** ⟳

These little pasta rounds are filled with such a succulent combination of vegetables that no extra sauce is required. Serve with mixed leaves or a tomato and onion salad.

INGREDIENTS

butter, for greasing

1 quantity Basic Pasta Dough
(see page 13)

plain flour, for dusting

85 g/3 oz freshly grated
Parmesan cheese

FILLING

125 ml/4 fl oz olive oil

1 red onion, chopped

3 garlic cloves, chopped

2 large aubergines, cut into chunks

3 large courgettes, cut into chunks

6 beef tomatoes, peeled, deseeded
and roughly chopped

1 large green pepper, deseeded
and diced

1 large red pepper, deseeded
and diced

1 tbsp sun-dried tomato paste

1 tbsp shredded fresh basil

salt and pepper

NUTRITIONAL INFORMATION

Calories 684

Protein 23g

Carbohydrate 59g

Sugars 15g

Fat 42g

Saturates 10g

variation

You can use this filling for most pasta shapes, such as ravioli (see page 79) or tortellini (see page 80).

cook's tip

If the filling seems too sloppy after cooking, boil uncovered for 1–2 minutes to reduce slightly. Make sure that any unused dough is covered with a tea towel to prevent it drying out.

1 Preheat the oven to 200°C/400°F/Gas Mark 6. To make the filling, heat the olive oil in a large heavy-based saucepan. Add the onion and garlic and cook over a low heat, stirring occasionally, for 5 minutes, or until softened. Add the aubergines, courgettes, tomatoes, green and red peppers, sun-dried tomato

paste and basil. Season to taste with salt and pepper, cover and simmer gently, stirring occasionally, for 20 minutes.

2 Lightly grease an ovenproof dish with butter. Roll out the Pasta Dough on a lightly floured work surface and stamp out 7.5-cm/3-inch rounds with a plain pastry cutter. Place a

spoonful of the vegetable filling on each round. Dampen the edges slightly and fold the pasta rounds over, pressing together to seal.

3 Bring a large saucepan of lightly salted water to the boil. Add the agnolotti, in batches if necessary, return to the boil and cook for 3–4 minutes. Remove with a

slotted spoon, drain and transfer to the dish. Sprinkle with the Parmesan cheese and bake in the preheated oven for 20 minutes. Serve immediately.

spinach & ricotta ravioli

serves 4   **prep: 25 mins, plus 1 hr resting**   **cook: 15 mins**

A favourite Italian combination, spinach and ricotta appears in many guises from roulades to crêpes, but it is never more delicious than as a filling for home-made pasta.

INGREDIENTS

350 g/12 oz spinach leaves, coarse stalks removed

225 g/8 oz ricotta cheese

55 g/2 oz freshly grated Parmesan cheese

1 egg, lightly beaten

pinch of freshly grated nutmeg

pepper

1 quantity Spinach Pasta Dough (see page 13)

plain flour, for dusting

TO SERVE

freshly grated Parmesan cheese

Cheese Sauce (see page 36) or Tomato & Red Pepper Sauce (see page 147)

NUTRITIONAL INFORMATION

Calories 434

Protein 25g

Carbohydrate 42g

Sugars 4g

Fat 19g

Saturates 8g

variation

Replace the Spinach Pasta Dough with either plain or tomato-flavoured dough and add 1 tablespoon of chopped fresh parsley to the filling in Step 2.

cook's tip

When cutting the ravioli into squares, use a special pasta cutter available from kitchenware shops. Alternatively, you can use a sharp knife.

1 To make the filling, place the spinach in a heavy-based saucepan with just the water clinging to the leaves after washing, then cover and cook over a low heat for 5 minutes, or until wilted. Drain well and squeeze out as much moisture as possible. Leave to cool, then chop finely.

2 Beat the ricotta cheese until smooth, then stir in the spinach, Parmesan cheese and egg and season to taste with nutmeg and pepper.

3 Divide the Pasta Dough in half and roll out on a lightly floured work surface. Make the ravioli (see page 79, Step 2), filling them with the spinach and ricotta mixture. Cut the ravioli into squares and place on a floured tea towel. Leave to rest for 1 hour.

4 Bring a large heavy-based saucepan of lightly salted water to the boil, add the ravioli, in batches, return to the boil and cook for 5 minutes. Remove with a slotted spoon and drain on kitchen paper. Transfer to a warmed serving dish and serve immediately, sprinkled with Parmesan cheese and/or a sauce, if you like.

penne with creamy mushrooms

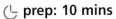 cook: 20 mins   prep: 10 mins   serves 4

NUTRITIONAL INFORMATION

Calories 780

Protein 15g

Carbohydrate 71g

Sugars 7g

Fat 50g

Saturates 21g

variation

Replace the shallots with a small onion, sliced, and substitute the pasta with other short pasta, such as farfalle, fusilli or rigatoni.

This quick and easy dish would make a wonderful midweek supper, whether or not you are a vegetarian family. Serve with fresh ciabatta, if you like.

INGREDIENTS

55 g/2 oz butter

1 tbsp olive oil

6 shallots, sliced

450 g/1 lb chestnut mushrooms, sliced

salt and pepper

1 tsp plain flour

150 ml/5 fl oz double cream or

panna da cucina

2 tbsp port

115 g/4 oz sun-dried tomatoes in oil, drained and chopped

pinch freshly grated nutmeg

350 g/12 oz dried penne

2 tbsp chopped fresh flat-leaved parsley

cook's tip

Nutmeg is used widely in Italian cooking as it has a fragrant, sweet aroma. Use freshly grated nutmeg rather than ground, which rapidly deteriorates. Store nutmeg in an airtight container.

1 Melt the butter with the olive oil in a large heavy-based frying pan. Add the shallots and cook over a low heat, stirring occasionally, for 4–5 minutes, or until softened. Add the mushrooms and cook over a low heat for a further 2 minutes. Season to taste with salt and pepper, sprinkle in the flour and cook, stirring, for 1 minute.

2 Remove the frying pan from the heat and gradually stir in the cream and port. Return to the heat, add the sun-dried tomatoes and grated nutmeg and cook over a low heat, stirring occasionally, for 8 minutes.

3 Meanwhile, bring a large heavy-based saucepan of lightly salted water to the boil. Add the pasta, return to the boil and cook for 8–10 minutes, or until tender but still firm to the bite. Drain the pasta well and add to the mushroom sauce. Cook for 3 minutes, then transfer to a warmed serving dish. Sprinkle with the chopped parsley and serve immediately.

tagliatelle with sun-dried tomatoes

serves 4   **prep: 10 mins** ⏱   **cook: 10 mins** ⏱

Quick, easy, utterly delicious and full of sunshine colours and flavours, this is the perfect dish for any occasion, whether it is a family supper or an informal dinner party.

INGREDIENTS

350 g/12 oz dried tagliatelle

1 tbsp olive oil

2 pieces of sun-dried tomatoes in oil, drained and thinly sliced

2 tbsp sun-dried tomato paste

225 ml/8 fl oz dry white wine

55 g/2 oz radicchio leaves, shredded

salt and pepper

3 spring onions, thinly sliced

3 tbsp lightly toasted pine kernels

NUTRITIONAL INFORMATION	
Calories	.494
Protein	.13g
Carbohydrate	.68g
Sugars	.5g
Fat	.17g
Saturates	.2g

cook's tip

To toast pine kernels, place them in a heavy-based or non-stick dry frying pan and cook over a medium heat, stirring and tossing constantly, for 1–2 minutes, until golden.

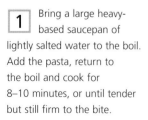

1 Bring a large heavy-based saucepan of lightly salted water to the boil. Add the pasta, return to the boil and cook for 8–10 minutes, or until tender but still firm to the bite.

2 Meanwhile, heat half the olive oil in a large heavy-based frying pan. Add the tomatoes and sun-dried tomato paste and stir in the wine. Simmer over a low heat, stirring constantly, or until slightly reduced. Stir in the radicchio and season to taste with salt and pepper.

3 Drain the pasta and transfer to a warmed serving dish. Add the remaining olive oil and toss well with 2 forks. Top with the sun-dried tomato sauce and toss lightly again, then sprinkle with the spring onions and toasted pine kernels and serve immediately.

linguine with wild mushrooms

 cook: 20 mins   prep: 15 mins   serves 4

Use any combination of your favourite mushrooms, such as chanterelles, field, oyster and chestnut, or use just one well-flavoured variety, such as ceps, horn of plenty or hedgehog fungus.

NUTRITIONAL INFORMATION

Calories 600

Protein 19g

Carbohydrate 72g

Sugars 5g

Fat 28g

Saturates 17g

INGREDIENTS

55 g/2 oz butter

1 onion, chopped

1 garlic clove, finely chopped

350 g/12 oz wild mushrooms, sliced

350 g/12 oz dried linguine

300 ml/10 fl oz crème fraîche

2 tbsp shredded fresh basil leaves, plus extra to garnish

4 tbsp freshly grated Parmesan cheese, plus extra to serve

salt and pepper

cook's tip

If you pick wild mushrooms yourself, make sure that you can identify them correctly, as many inedible or even toxic mushrooms closely resemble a number of edible varieties.

1 Melt the butter in a large heavy-based frying pan. Add the onion and garlic and cook over a low heat for 5 minutes, or until softened. Add the mushrooms and cook, stirring occasionally, for a further 10 minutes.

2 Meanwhile, bring a large heavy-based saucepan of lightly salted water to the boil. Add the pasta, return to the boil and cook for 8–10 minutes, or until tender but still firm to the bite.

3 Stir the crème fraîche, basil and Parmesan cheese into the mushroom mixture and season to taste with salt and pepper. Cover and heat through gently for 1–2 minutes. Drain the pasta and transfer to a warmed serving dish. Add the mushroom mixture and toss lightly. Garnish with extra basil and serve immediately with extra Parmesan cheese.

penne with mixed beans

This is a useful – and versatile – store cupboard dish that makes a filling and delicious meal for both vegetarians and vegans which can be whipped up in only a matter of minutes.

INGREDIENTS

1 tbsp olive oil

1 onion, chopped

1 garlic clove, finely chopped

1 carrot, finely chopped

1 celery stick, finely chopped

425 g/15 oz canned mixed beans, drained and rinsed

225 ml/8 fl oz passata

1 tbsp chopped fresh chervil, plus extra leaves to garnish

salt and pepper

350 g/12 oz dried penne

NUTRITIONAL INFORMATION

Calories 366

Protein 14g

Carbohydrate 72g

Sugars 7g

Fat 5g

Saturates 0g

variation

Most canned pulses, with the exception of lentils, could be used separately or in combination. Try borlotti or red kidneys beans, flageolets or chickpeas.

1 Heat the olive oil in a large heavy-based frying pan. Add the onion, garlic, carrot and celery and cook over a low heat, stirring occasionally, for 5 minutes, or until the onion has softened.

2 Add the mixed beans, passata and chopped chervil to the frying pan and season the mixture to taste with salt and pepper. Cover and simmer gently for 15 minutes.

3 Meanwhile, bring a large heavy-based saucepan of lightly salted water to the boil. Add the pasta, return to the boil and cook for 8–10 minutes, or until tender but still firm to the bite. Drain the pasta and transfer to a warmed serving dish. Add the mixed bean sauce, toss well and serve immediately, garnished with extra chervil.

tagliarini with courgettes

cook: 25 mins   prep: 15 mins   serves 4

This dish is ideal to serve on a hot summer's day as it is full of the sunshine flavours of the Mediterranean. You can serve the Parmesan cheese separately so everyone can help themselves.

NUTRITIONAL INFORMATION

Calories 555

Protein 22g

Carbohydrate 77g

Sugars 7g

Fat 20g

Saturates 6g

INGREDIENTS

4 tbsp olive oil

1 red onion, chopped

1 garlic clove, finely chopped

500 g/1 lb 2 oz courgettes, diced

2 beef tomatoes, peeled, deseeded and finely chopped

salt

pinch of cayenne pepper

1 tbsp shredded fresh basil leaves

350 g/12 oz dried tagliarini

85 g/3 oz freshly grated Parmesan cheese, to serve

variation

Use spaghetti instead of the tagliarini and replace the basil with the same amount of chopped fresh flat-leaved parsley.

1 Heat the oil in a large heavy-based frying pan. Add the onion and garlic and cook over a low heat, stirring occasionally, for 5 minutes, or until softened. Add the courgettes and cook, stirring, for a further 3 minutes.

2 Add the tomatoes and season to taste with salt and cayenne pepper. Stir in the basil, cover and cook for 10–15 minutes, or until all the vegetables are tender.

3 Meanwhile, bring a large heavy-based saucepan of lightly salted water to the boil. Add the pasta, return to the boil and cook for 8–10 minutes, or until tender but still firm to the bite. Drain the pasta and transfer to a warmed serving dish. Add the courgette and tomato sauce and toss well. Sprinkle with the Parmesan cheese and serve immediately.

orecchiette salad with pears & stilton

serves 4   **prep: 15 mins** ⏲   **cook: 10 mins** ⏲

A classic combination in British cooking, pears and blue cheese, form the basis of this unusual salad, which could serve as a main course for four people or as an accompaniment or starter for six.

INGREDIENTS

250 g/9 oz dried orecchiette	1 red onion, sliced
1 head of radicchio, torn into pieces	1 carrot, grated
1 oakleaf lettuce, torn into pieces	8 fresh basil leaves
2 pears	55 g/2 oz lamb's lettuce
3 tbsp lemon juice	4 tbsp olive oil
250 g/9 oz Stilton cheese, diced	3 tbsp white wine vinegar
55 g/2 oz chopped walnuts	salt and pepper
4 tomatoes, quartered	

NUTRITIONAL INFORMATION

Calories	.766
Protein	.27g
Carbohydrate	.66g
Sugars	.19g
Fat	.46g
Saturates	.17g

variation

Substitute the oakleaf lettuce with escarole and replace the lamb's lettuce with rocket or watercress, if you prefer.

cook's tip

The easiest way to emulsify an oil and vinegar dressing is to put the ingredients in a screw-top jar, secure the lid and shake vigorously. Otherwise, whisk well in a bowl or jug.

1 Bring a large heavy-based saucepan of lightly salted water to the boil. Add the pasta, return to the boil and cook for 8–10 minutes, or until tender but still firm to the bite. Drain, refresh in a bowl of cold water and drain again.

2 Place the radicchio and oakleaf lettuce leaves in a salad bowl. Halve the pears, remove the cores and dice the flesh. Toss the diced pear with 1 tablespoon of lemon juice in a small bowl to prevent discoloration. Top the salad with the Stilton, walnuts, pears, pasta, tomatoes, onion slices and grated carrot. Add the basil and lamb's lettuce.

3 Mix the remaining lemon juice and the olive oil and vinegar together in a jug, then season to taste with salt and pepper. Pour the dressing over the salad, toss and serve.

pasta salad with curry dressing

serves 4 **prep: 10 mins** **cook: 10 mins**

You can make this salad well in advance and it would be a good accompaniment to serve at a barbecue party.

INGREDIENTS

115 g/4 oz dried farfalle

4–5 large lettuce leaves

1 green pepper, deseeded and chopped

1 red pepper, deseeded and chopped

2 tbsp snipped fresh chives

115 g/4 oz button mushrooms, chopped

DRESSING

2 tsp curry powder

1 tbsp caster sugar

125 ml/4 fl oz sunflower oil

50 ml/2 fl oz white wine vinegar

1 tbsp single cream

NUTRITIONAL INFORMATION

Calories 356

Protein 5g

Carbohydrate 28g

Sugars 7g

Fat 26g

Saturates 3g

variation

Replace the farfalle with other pasta shapes such as penne, fusilli or conchiglie and use chestnut mushrooms instead of the buttons, if you prefer.

cook's tip

If making this salad a few hours in advance, do not add the curry dressing to the salad until just before serving, otherwise it may go soggy.

1 Bring a large heavy-based saucepan of lightly salted water to the boil. Add the pasta, return to the boil and cook for 8–10 minutes, or until tender but still firm to the bite. Drain, rinse in a bowl of cold water and drain again.

2 Line a large salad bowl with the lettuce leaves and tip in the pasta. Add the green and red peppers, chives and mushrooms.

3 To make the dressing, place the curry powder and sugar in a small bowl and gradually stir in the oil, vinegar and cream. Whisk well and pour the dressing over the salad. Toss lightly and serve.

warm pasta salad

 cook: 10 mins   prep: 10 mins   serves 4

NUTRITIONAL INFORMATION

Calories 415

Protein 10g

Carbohydrate 44g

Sugars 4g

Fat 23g

Saturates 4g

variation

For an alternative dressing, replace 1 tablespoon of the olive oil with hazelnut oil and replace the white wine vinegar with raspberry vinegar.

Serve this salad on its own for a light lunch or as a substantial accompaniment to chicken or fish.

INGREDIENTS

225 g/8 oz dried farfalle or other pasta shapes

6 pieces of sun-dried tomato in oil, drained and chopped

4 spring onions, chopped

55 g/2 oz rocket, shredded

½ cucumber, deseeded and diced

salt and pepper

2 tbsp freshly grated Parmesan cheese

DRESSING

4 tbsp olive oil

1 tbsp white wine vinegar

½ tsp caster sugar

1 tsp Dijon mustard

salt and pepper

4 fresh basil leaves, finely shredded

cook's tip

It makes it easier to toss the pasta if you use 2 forks or 2 dessertspoons, and before adding the dressing to the salad, whisk it again until emulsified. Add the dressing just before serving.

1 To make the dressing, whisk the olive oil, vinegar, sugar and mustard together in a jug. Season to taste with salt and pepper and stir in the basil.

2 Bring a large heavy-based saucepan of lightly salted water to the boil. Add the pasta, return to the boil and cook for 8–10 minutes, or until tender but still firm to the bite. Drain and transfer to a salad bowl. Add the dressing and toss well.

3 Add the tomatoes, spring onions, rocket and cucumber, season to taste with salt and pepper and toss. Sprinkle with the Parmesan cheese and serve warm.

pasta niçoise

serves 4 **prep: 15 mins, plus 15 mins cooling** **cook: 15–20 mins**

This classic French salad, bursting with flavours of the Mediterranean, is given additional substance, texture and colour with the addition of pasta, making it a filling summer dish.

INGREDIENTS

115 g/4 oz green beans, cut into
5-cm/2-inch lengths
225 g/8 oz dried fusilli tricolore
100 ml/3½ fl oz olive oil
2 tuna steaks, about 350 g/12 oz each
salt and pepper
6 cherry tomatoes, halved
55 g/2 oz black olives, stoned and halved
6 canned anchovies, drained
and chopped
3 tbsp chopped fresh flat-leaved parsley
2 tbsp lemon juice
8–10 radicchio leaves

NUTRITIONAL INFORMATION

Calories 636

Protein 50g

Carbohydrate 44g

Sugars 3g

Fat 30g

Saturates 5g

cook's tip

Brushing or spraying the griddle pan with oil helps prevent the food sticking. After cooking, leave the griddle pan to cool, do not plunge it into cold water as this may warp the pan.

1 Bring a large heavy-based saucepan of lightly salted water to the boil. Add the beans, reduce the heat and cook for 5–6 minutes. Remove with a slotted spoon and refresh in a bowl of cold water. Drain well. Add the pasta to the same saucepan, return to the boil and cook for 8–10 minutes, or until tender but still firm to the bite.

2 Meanwhile, brush a griddle pan with olive oil and heat until smoking. Season the tuna with salt and pepper to taste and brush both sides with olive oil. Cook over a medium heat for 2 minutes on each side, or until cooked to your liking, then remove from the griddle pan and reserve.

3 Drain the pasta well and tip it into a bowl. Add the beans, tomatoes, olives, anchovies, parsley, lemon juice and remaining oil and season to taste with salt and pepper. Toss well and leave to cool. Remove and discard any skin from the tuna and slice thickly.

4 Gently mix the tuna into the pasta salad. Line a large salad bowl with the radicchio leaves, spoon in the salad and serve.

pasta salad with nuts & dolcelatte

⏲ **cook: 10 mins**　　　　　🕐 **prep: 10 mins**　　　　　**serves 4**

Choose a colourful selection of salad leaves with a range of flavours, such as lollo rosso, rocket, radicchio and frisée, to provide an appealing background to the pasta, nuts and blue cheese.

NUTRITIONAL INFORMATION	
Calories	.765
Protein	.17g
Carbohydrate	.44g
Sugars	.4g
Fat	.56g
Saturates	.17g

INGREDIENTS

225 g/8 oz dried farfalle

2 tbsp walnut oil

4 tbsp safflower oil

2 tbsp balsamic vinegar

salt and pepper

280 g/10 oz mixed salad leaves

225 g/8 oz dolcelatte cheese, diced

115 g/4 oz walnuts, halved and toasted

1 Bring a large heavy-based saucepan of lightly salted water to the boil. Add the pasta, return to the boil and cook for 8–10 minutes, or until tender but still firm to the bite. Drain and refresh in a bowl of cold water. Drain again.

2 Mix the walnut oil, safflower oil and vinegar together in a jug, whisking well, and season to taste with salt and pepper.

3 Arrange the salad leaves in a large serving bowl. Top with the pasta, dolcelatte cheese and walnuts. Pour the dressing over the salad, toss lightly and serve.

variation

Substitute hazelnuts for the walnuts and hazelnut oil for the walnut oil, if you prefer. Replace the farfalle with penne rigate or fusilli.

index

index

index